Rutl 

Dedicated to:

SUSAN, OLIVIA, URSULA, LOUIS, BRITTANY AND KRISTINA

And

Emma, Beau and Dylan

....

ACKNOWLEDGEMENTS:

I WOULD LIKE TO EXPRESS MY SINCERE THANKS AND LOVE TO MARIAN MCINTIRE AND MIDGE KERN, MY WONDERFUL NONAGENARIAN FRIENDS FOR GIVING ME INSIGHT INTO THE LIFE AND TIMES OF THE PIONEER LIFESTYLE DURING THE EARLY YEARS OF THE TWENTIETH CENTURY. THANKS TOO FOR YOUR ENCOURAGEMENT AND SUPPORT.

Also, I'd like to express my love and appreciation to those who patiently edited my little book. To Doris Rosenberg, Dee Olson, her sister, Marcella, Jeanette Colley, Lynn Rideout and Marian Bucholz. I give my thanks to Jan, Dodee and Michael as well. May we walk along together through many more pages of life.

FORWARD:

Sleepy Eye is the fictionized name of Bertha, Minnesota, not to be confused with the *real* Sleepy Eye in the southern part of the state. – The names of relatives and friends have been changed to protect their identities.

I was #15 in a clan of 17 children and am writing only what I observed. It all took place many years ago. What I could not remember I have embellished on making the work a memoir/novel. The book is largely true except for the last section in the chapter "Good Neighbors." It was such fun writing that I couldn't leave it out. Happy reading!

Ruth R. Haase

CONTENTS

Sixteen Siblings

CHAPTER I CLARA

Dear Reader/friend: I was born into a family of no fewer than seventeen children. That sounds unreal until I tell you that my father, Edgar M. Rosenburg, was widowed and took a second wife. His first wife, Clara, presented him with six progeny, five girls and one boy. The eldest, Johannah, had just celebrated her thirteenth birthday when her mother was killed in a farm accident early in the year 1913. Clara had worked outside along with her husband tending the animals on the ranch.

Some seven decades later I inquired as to how Clara had died. Her children were up into their sixties and seventies and had forgotten a lot by that time. But that sort of thing had never been talked about in those days. It was swept under the rug and perhaps that was all for the better.....

Some of my half-sisters thought Clara had been dragged to death behind a team of horses, something that occurred from time to time in plains country, near the quiet little hamlet of Sleepy Eye, Minnesota. I heard another story: this account had Clara in a stall with a young bull feeding him grain. The youngish bull had gotten mad and she had been *bunted to death! Either way it was tragic beyond words!*

The farmers believed in having large families to help on the farm, and legend has it that poor Clara was *five months pregnant* at the time of her demise!

This was prairie country, with small farms close together, and stands of hardwood trees: oak, maple, birch and poplar. The Rosenburg Ranch was probably the largest farm in the area at 400 acres, half a section.

After Clara's death my mom went to work for dad as a "hired girl". Subsequently they wed. She Anna, never one to be outdone proudly produced eleven more babies, seven daughters and four sons. No such thing as the 'population explosion' there was at the time and I think my dad felt it was his pleasure to help populate the county. Many of the farmers of that day had offspring in the two-digit numbers. That's the way it was.

I'm down towards the end of this mob, #15. I was christened Ruth Augusta, but I go by Rudy or "Rootkin", my mother's pet nickname for me. My dad was fifty-six and my mother was forty when I came along, and my dad was having so much fun he 'begat' two more: my little sister, Carrie, and child #17, Mickey.

Dad was a commanding figure just a shade under six foot tall, with the Germanic blue eyes and big bones. With sandy hair, and a chiseled chin he must have been a striking figure in his younger days. A dairy farmer, he would have preferred to bring more boys into the world but he welcomed these winsome little lassies.

Albert, Clara's only son, was a lad of nine when his mother died, but he followed his daddy along and learned to be a real help on the ranch early in life. The state of Minnesota was a fertile farming frontier at the time; still is.

This left my mother, Anna, stepping into this job of seven mouths to feed three times a day, not an easy task for the most devoted soul. I say seven because my Mom never ate anything, sustaining herself on coffee with cream.

After Clara's death my Dad looked around in Sleepy Eye, three and a half miles due west of the ranch for a 'hired girl' to care for his six little darlings. Unable to find just the right female there he hitched up horse and buggy traveling the twenty-eight miles to Parkers Prairie looking for this wonder woman.

After asking around in Parkers for an hour he finally heard of one Anna Greske, who might be looking for work. Edgar found the Greske residence, a small farm just outside of town and announced his business to the lady of the house.

Mama Greske went upstairs to speak to her daughter. Anna straightened up, splashed icy-cold water on her face from the porcelain water pitcher, ran a brush through her tangled hair and tried to put a smile on her face. She took a deep breath and wobbled down the stairs, hoping this prospective employer wouldn't notice how red and puffy her eyes were from all the weeping and depression she had recently suffered.

She told Mr. Rosenburg about "working out" in Hillsboro, North Dakota and Thief River Falls in Minnesota. ("T'eef River"). Having been born in Germany, my mom was never able to pronounce her th's. She had had lots of experience, having been employed by the Hennings as a "hired girl". Also working for Dr. and Mrs. Penney, and the Vaseners as a housekeeper. *And she had the important thing: credentials.*

When this prospective employer mentioned having six children to care for, Anna perked up. She had been around kids a lot in her housekeeping days, and looked forward to having a batch of babies of her own someday. She thought this job would be good preparation towards that goal. She was feeling better already.

Now she went straightaway and packed her bag. She put in three or four cotton housedresses, two long-sleeved wool sweaters opening down the front, two "good" dresses for church she had worn when dating her boyfriend, now deceased, and lovely hand-embroidered underskirts and bloomers.

This was the suitcase she had bought when she worked for the Hennings, her first job. The beat-up medium-size bag was not much more than heavy dark brown cardboard, with metal reinforcements at the corners, straps going around and buckles to close. Anna hurriedly packed. This job offer was what she had been praying for.

She could scarcely believe her good fortune! That God would send someone right to her door offering her a job, much the kind of work she had done before. Even though He had seen fit for her boyfriend to go, here and now God was giving her this new opportunity, essentially laying the job in her lap! She bit her lip and closed her eyes for a second at the very thought of it.

What a change from all the depression she had been suffering! She hadn't been outside for weeks. Now Anna went to the closet and found her brown coat and tam. Her coat felt loose on her frame since she had lost so much weight, being cooped up in her room for so long unable to eat. She wound a threadbare red scarf around her neck and went back with Mr. Rosenburg to his home and his children on Chokecherry Lane.

Edgar and Anna stopped at the little cafe in Parkers Prairie for a bite to eat. Anna ordered cherry pie and coffee with cream while her new employer enjoyed his lemon pie and coffee. (The cream was served in small glass 'vessels' placed on the table.) The quick stop at the cafe was just what Anna needed to bolster her spirits for the trip back to the Rosenburg Ranch. Edgar helped Anna up into the seat beside him.

She may have been a tad apprehensive after spending so much time in a darkened room. She might have had reservations about what she was getting herself into. -- Anna tried to make conversation on the trip back to the ranch but when she talked the words came out stiff and clumsy, so she remained silent for most of the way. -- That would change when she began to feel better because she could chatter up a storm.

No doubt Edgar noticed her medium build and strong hands. He probably thought she was used to hard work. I don't think he noticed how pretty Anna was, her slender figure, wavy hair and lovely brown eyes. He was interested only in a housekeeper besides a nanny and confidante for his brood.

Sleepy Eye was a clean-looking hamlet with white houses. The village had the usual businesses besides the post office: a general store, the mercantile store, the First National Bank and the Land O Lakes Creamery. Also a couple eateries, an undertaker and the ever-present saloon. A beauty salon was located in the residential section of town. I believe the little town of 454 people was incorporated at that time.

When they arrived at the ranch the sun was at 3 o'clock. The big farmhouse sat away back from the road on a rise. A large lawn bordered the gravel road. The lilac trees were beginning to blossom, their scent wafting through the spring air. The place was pregnant with the smell of spring, chirping meadowlarks, and nature at its best.

In my mind's eye I see my handsome Father running around the buggy, helping Anna down from the carriage. By the time she had disembarked the children had assembled themselves according to age on a long bench Edgar had made. Johannah, the eldest, stood and bowed deeply introducing herself. She held her hand out to Martha, next in line. "This is Marty," she said pleasantly. Marty placed a wildflower on the ground, skipped around it and went back in place. She introduced Selma. Now Selma (Sally), always the diplomat, smiled broadly showing off white even teeth.

Albert, the only son, stepped forward, saluting. “My name is Albert,” he said, then did a handstand for this new lady. Helen had dimples. She ambled towards Anna, winking at her. Lastly came little Hildeguard with freckles across her nose, her dark hair in pigtails. She walked slowly over to Anna and took her hand with a toothless grin. Anna could hardly hear her she spoke so softly, but thought the little girl said: “Hildie”.

As Edgar ushered Anna through the back door and into the kitchen five of the children followed like ducklings padding behind a mama duck. Johannah hung back. She liked this new 'housemother' already; yet she wanted to see more of her and how she related to her sisters. Johannah had been like a mama tiger where her siblings were concerned.

She had taught the smaller girls how to wash dishes in a pan on the stove, and instructed Marty and Sally to look for cobwebs in the corners when they swept. At thirteen Johannah was at the threshold of becoming a real lady, and she had always been mature for her age. She delegated jobs to her sisters, and every one of the girls did her part cleaning up after herself.

She, Marty and Sally took time out to talk to the smaller girls, Helen and Hildie. They told them in simple terms that their dear mother had gone to heaven, a better place. Even though the older girls were still grieving themselves they tried to keep the little girls occupied so they wouldn't have time to brood over their mother's death. They were sensible young ladies.....

CHAPTER II FRED ZINTER

Fast forward to the mid-forties. We are now residing in Sleepy Eye proper, having moved into town when I was in 7th grade. Only three of us kids are still living at home: Carrie, Mickey and I. Carrie and I are doing homework on the dining table in the evening. It was a rare night that neither of us was baby-sitting. My mother, always skinny as a nail, came in from the kitchen to "warm her back" by the oil burning furnace in the dining room. Often she'd get this faraway look in her eyes. In a high-pitched voice she'd say: "He was so sweet on me!" Then she danced a little jig just to think of it.

My dad sat in his easy chair just through the archway in the parlor smoking his pipe and listening to the table-model radio. Upon hearing this from his wife of thirty-three years who had borne him eleven young he'd raise his eyebrows a little, grin a little, and go on listening to "Amos 'n Andy". Now in his mid-seventies he joked to us often during high school: "The first hundred years are the hardest."

In my reverie I see him knocking his pipe sharply against the table that the radio sat on. Then he'd empty the stale tobacco into one of my mother's potted plants, hitting the pipe so the used tobacco fell gently into the soil. I don't know whether she ever caught on or not.

Carrie and I had heard my mom say: "He was so sweet on me!" over and over through the years. She always danced the little jig. I used to wonder what the jig was all about. Now I know it was because her boyfriend -- a beau she'd had before she met my dad -- had loved to dance. They never missed a dance at the pavilion in Parkers Prairie.

That was all we knew until *two generations later* when my daughter, Stephanie, a career girl of twenty-six, accompanied me from the state of Washington back to Sleepy Eye. We were there in Minnesota to attend a get-together and say our Goodbyes to Mickey, the youngest child. He was dying of cancer at the age of forty-nine. -- The reunion had been planned for the 4th of July weekend. Stephanie and I had our plane tickets, but as I had feared would happen, Mickey didn't live that long; passing away in June.

Stephanie and I kept with our original plans. So when we arrived on the 4th we visited with Debbie, Mickey's widow, in the St. Paul area and were able to meet some of her children. Then we drove up to Sleepy Eye, staying at my mom's.

Anna Greske Rosenburg, my mother, *now ninety-two,* still lived in her own home. She decided the time was ripe to divulge this true-life legend. Dad had passed away a number of years before. He had lived to the ripe old age of 83, and Anna was sixteen years younger. Now after Dad was gone she still had a lot of living to do. She was made of some durable stuff.

Stephanie and I slept in the screened-in porch as the Minnesota night lived up to its reputation: hot and humid. Upon awakening I heard my Mother telling Steph about her first love, one Fred Zinter. Anna and Stephanie were talking quietly enjoying their coffee while munching poppy seed muffins. My Mom was settled in her brown wicker couch in the dining room telling this true story of the man who had loved her so dearly he would have given her "the moon" to have her for his bride. *She had kept the story hidden within her psyche over seven decades.*

My mother was going on ninety-three but her face and her active lifestyle belied her age, and her hair, though not as dark as it once was, still was more pepper than salt.

Her soft-green sleeveless gingham dress showed off her slender upper-arms, just right for the July Midwest morning. She drank her coffee the way she liked it best, with lots of milk, almost half coffee and half milk. Going to the kitchen I found the coffee pot my mom had brewed fresh for the day. At this stage of her life she always had four or five different-sized percolators sitting on the gas range. I felt for the hot one, refilled Stephanie's and mom's cups, pouring myself a cup. Pulling out a straight - backed chair from the dining table I sat by my daughter.

Antiques stood all over the dining room and parlor. Next to the wicker couch, in a corner of the room, stood Mom's old console treadle sewing machine she had used to make doll dresses for Carrie and me. She had placed my high school graduation picture on the sewing machine, and there it sat for thirty-six years. I had worn a yellow blouse and put pin curls in my blonde hair the night before giving it a nice curl. My makeup had been only lipstick. Just above my picture hung a hexagon mirror with a decorative border.

The sun filtered through gossamer crisscross curtains making lovely reflections on the reddish-purple wallpaper. My mother loved the color red and used shades of it in her attire and in decorating her home. -- Her buffet, close to mint condition, stood in the next corner; while next to the archway leading into the front room was her china hutch with the curved glass doors.

Lush ferns sat on plant stands by the windows. Her favorites were the Boston ferns, but she also had lovely asparagus ferns. The long lacy ferns held a special place in her heart. My Mom always worried that when I came home with all my kids, four at the time -- including twins -- they might touch the tips of the fronds turning the edges brown. It didn't happen that way. My kids were never there long enough to damage her wonderful ferns; and they were not rowdy. If I sound a little resentful, Reader/friend, it's because I was.

Around the dining table several rockers crowded the room. Mom collected rockers in all shapes and sizes. Mirrors on the wall and rockers on the hardwood floor, she was happy there. She loved her rockers although she didn't find time to sit in them, constantly working in her home and rarely sitting down until going to bed at night.

As I sat down I kept hearing the name Fred Zinter. My mom had been quite taken by this man, a boyfriend she'd had before she met my Father. Fred Z. had had a burning crush on Anna which developed into a full-blown love affair. "Why don't you start over, Ma," said I. "I didn't hear the first part of the story."

She pushed her hair back behind her left ear. Wrinkling her brow she said: "Ach, let me t'ink. I don't hardly know where to begin... He loved to run his fingers t'rough my hair, I remember dat. We had been seeing each other over a year now, and I had met his mother and his old-maid sisters, Bessie and Tessie. And had visited at their home different times."

A soft glow came into mom's dark eyes as she concentrated on her first love. The words came haltingly at first, as if she didn't want to open this secret file which had lain untouched almost three-quarters of a century. Apparently she thought the story should be dusted off and told to someone. She took another sip of coffee; then smoothed her dress over her knees. Anna now gave us some insight into this man, Fred. "Let me see, where should I... er, ach... He was nice enough to look at, with dark hair and dark eyes and t'ick eyebrows. And a nice smile. Freddie was always smiling."

My mom had a thick German accent, Reader/friend, which she never did lose. The word 'thick' was always "t'ick" and 'the' she pronounced “de”. ‘Through’ was “t’rough”; she said “valk” for ‘walk’ and ‘yes’ was “jah”, but to make easy reading I’ll put only a few words in her native accent. With that for a preface the ‘Queen’s English’ will be used for the most part.

“He was a wonderful dancer; with his slight frame his feet just flew off de floor. He whirled me t’rough de polka like I was a wind-up doll!" Mom couldn't help but laugh. Stephanie and I looked at each other and smiled.

"Freddie and I walked hand in hand all over town, Parkers Prairie. I was five foot five and he was scarcely an inch taller. We both had dark hair and brown eyes. Newcomers in town t’ought we were brother and sister. When we went dancing Freddie wore a brown pin-stripe suit, and a neat little vest with white shirt. He parted his hair down de middle. In winter he wore spats on his wing-tip shoes. Jah, Freddie was quite a dresser. I t'ink dat’s what interested me in de first place."

Her eyes brightened as she thought about her first love. She sighed and covered her right hand over her left. Anna had thought about him now and then over the years, but had not revealed to her children anything about this man, Fred.

His memory had been tucked away in her heart all these years. Aunt Lena, Clara’s sister, and the other aunts knew the story but my Mom had never divulged a single word to us kids about the man who had had such passion for her.

"De dress I wore when we went dancing was a little black dress with a white lacy collar. Dat was high fashion back in de year nineteen hundred and twelve when I was a young lady of twenty-one. I can picture de details even now, small white buttons in de bodice and pleats down around my knees with pink ribbon going around by de pleats. I wanted to look nice for my beau without leading him on. My mind held a secret that I could not mention to Freddie." She coughed and reached in her pocket for her hankie; then took another swallow of coffee.

Anna described the "hobble skirt" of the early 1900's to her granddaughter. "Dese had gone out of style. De narrow skirts allowed a girl to take only small steps. I'd never liked dat style, and had never worn de hobble skirt.

And how Freddie loved to waltz! I looked forward to dose evenings out with dis man." She stopped to think about it and did a private giggle. This retelling seemed to be good medicine for her. "I danced every dance with Freddie, nearly breathless I was having such a good time! I can see myself gliding across de floor. My skirt length was just below the knee, just right for doing the polka. And like dat. De..." Her voice trailed off; then quickly came back: "Jah, de two of us carved quite a carpet." I knew my mom had a good sense of humor, but hadn't heard her humor in years.

My husband and our family lived in the state of Oregon while Stephanie and the boys were growing up, and hadn't gotten back to the Midwest except once every three years. We drove back east at least that often as we wanted our kids to know their grandparents. -- Now upon hearing this story I was glad my mom had gone dancing with Fred Zinter. My dad was a good man, but I certainly didn't see him taking her dancing. All he liked to do was talk politics and the news. He could talk politics as fast as a congressman.

Anna fingered her hankie while speaking. "Jah, I t'ink Mama and Papa figured it was just a matter of time before Freddie and I got married, giving the Greskes grandchildren.

And what fun Fred and I had at de basket-socials and pie-socials held at de country school! Dat was such a wonderful time in my life. I recollect de last basket-social of de season just before school let out in June. Dat was a big event in Parkers Prairie.

All de single men between seventeen and t'irty-five were present. 'Dese' men normally wore 'bib-overhaus' (overalls), but for de basket-social dey spiffed up in checkered shirts and jeans with leather belts." As my mother explained how it was back then, lean hardy men came to mind. They must have been a bodacious lot, ready for an exciting night out.

"How had these men gotten to the country school in the evening? Had they ridden on horseback?" I asked. "Ach," said Anna. "Freddie had a one-horse buggy. One or two drove de first automobiles. -- Henry Ford invented his 'Tin Lizzie' around 1908 or 1909, I t'ink. My memory isn't so good on dose t'ings, but most of de men drove horse-drawn buggies. One or two rode on horseback."

For the spring gala one year Anna recalled how she had decorated her basket. "I had gone all out dat year. My basket was pink with small red hearts. I always liked to draw, and had sketched a white cupid dat I glued on de basket handle." (I think she just wanted to see how high Freddie would go in the bidding.) "Inside de basket I folded two linen napkins.

Catalog sales were de new 'in' t'ing in de spring of nineteen, t'irteen. De dress I sent for was red and gray plaid." She chuckled again. She was happy to tell this fascinating story to her Granddaughter at this time in her life. "It's so funny. I can remember some of dose t'ings back den better den I can remember what I did yesterday!" She laughed. "Anyway, I had ordered de dress from de Sears and Roebuck catalog. And like dat.

When I put on de dress I had to take a deep, deep breath. Den two of my sisters, Emma and Louise, pulled tight on de laces in my corset. I had a small bust, but with de cinched waist my bust looked larger. Now I wear shoulder pads!" Anna laughed. Stephanie looked mystified. I whispered to her that my mom did indeed put soft shoulder pads in her bra to give her a little fullness in her breast. She began doing this in her 'later years'.

Jumping up to get the coffee pot, I poured coffee all around. When I poured for Anna, putting in lots of milk she said: "Fill it up!" I filled her cup with coffee almost to the rim, just so it wouldn't spill. Then she said: "Dere, dat's just right."

She continued her saga: "Rows of white ruffled trim ran along de square neckline of dat dress, and it had a gathered skirt." (She must have been a sight to behold.) "De young ladies of dose days wore ruffled petticoats with ruffled bloomers. Our undergarments were very feminine with ribbons, lace, and lots of embroidery. My stockings were gray silk. I knew I could not marry Freddie, but I wanted to look nice for him.

De high-button shoes had just gone out of style. My shoes were black pumps with a 2-inch heel and a grosgrain ribbon bow." She took a couple more bites of her muffin.

"De baskets came in all shapes and sizes and de auctioneer had fun describing dem. There were square baskets, round baskets and shoe boxes, in all different colors. De young suitors bid money dey could ill afford as dey set dere sights on de baskets.

When de bidding ceased Freddie put my basket over his arm. Den we went out beside de schoolhouse by de old oak trees where it was shady and cool. Fred brushed away de acorns and spread a worn beige blanket on de grass. I remember daffodils and hyacinths. Dey were so pretty dat year; de hyacinths smelled heavenly and de evening breeze was just right. It was a beautiful evening and Freddie always made me laugh.

De sun was just beginning to set. Fred had kissed me almost too much, but I couldn't have stopped him. He had said: 'De evening sun gives you a sparkle dat lights up your entire body!'" (Although how such a thing could happen what with all those petticoats I can't understand. From my conversations with Anna I have an idea that Fred was about as close to her as he could get within the law. And she no doubt tried to keep the wind from blowing her dress up, but sometimes one's two hands are not enough to go all the way around.)

"Freddie sniffed at de back of my neck. I t'ink his senses had found a favorite place dere." With her short hair follicles smelling so sweet he must have been captivated. "'You're de woman I cannot live without!' I heard him say. He chewed on my ear and kissed my neck. Den he kissed my hands. Ach, it was all so wonderful!" Anna laughed again. He certainly must have noticed her cinched-in waist and the ruffled neckline. "But he never went too far," Anna assured us. "He was always de gentleman. Dat was what I liked about him." She smiled.

"Finally Freddie finished nibbling on my ears," recalled this ninety-two-year-old. "He was like a puppy around me, sniffing and licking. Now he looked around for something with more substance. He opened de basket to find my specialty: fried chicken. Under his breath I heard him swoon: 'Life cannot be sweeter den dis!' Wonderful memories were being carved out, enough to last a lifetime, but I knew I could not marry dis man." Anna's eyes looked like they were going to tear up. Her 'Freddie years' had been a deeply emotional time in her life. She kept fingering her hankie and dabbed at her eyes.

Now she continued: "Soon other couples were seated on blankets eating their suppers from baskets. Fred always outbid de others where it concerned my basket. I guess he had found de woman of his dreams and notting would stand in his way to win me!" she laughed. "I t'ink he skimped in other ways so he had enough money for de basket-socials."

"Oh Grandma, this is so interesting!" commented Stephanie.

"T'ank you, Steph. umm... Later dat evening he walked me to my door. Dere he gave me a long drawn-out kiss. I really liked being close, but when he held me tight I had to pull back." She sniffled. "He was de nicest man I had ever met. Yet dat was as far as I wanted to go. He just wasn't de right man for me. And I didn't want to lead him on when I wasn't prepared to go de nineteen yards.

Sailing around de dance floor and picnics on blankets was one t'ing, but I didn't want to get too close. I promised myself I would tell him why in my own good time. Actually, I didn't know how serious he was. - Looking back on it I know Fred couldn't understand me. When he kissed me I acted uneasy. It must have been very difficult for him. And like dat."

Stephanie and I looked at each other, and our eyes met. We felt more like loving sisters, rather than mother and daughter. Since she was my only daughter -- four sons -- we had a close relationship.

Anna went on: "Freddie and I formed our own private path between my house and de Zinters on de edge of Parkers. It wound t'rough a woods of trees with small trunks, sometimes as t'ick as doghair. I pretended to fall on de path, running ahead with Freddie chasing not far behind. Some places de sun shone t'rough de trees, dappling on de path so pretty." Anna's eyes closed and she smiled as she brought it all back. It was a moment to cherish.

"I ran from one tree trunk to another maybe twenty feet away. I remember pretty wildflowers in de woods, and tiny violets. I liked de nice woodsy smell. Sometimes we looked for four-leaf clovers." They had had these lovely innocent encounters.

"A couple weeks after de final basket-social Freddie invited me to his home for dinner on Sunday after church. I had worn my red and gray plaid dress for de dinner.

We walked hand-in-hand directly to his house from church. As I crossed de t'reshold de aromas were really somet'ing! My nose almost smiled! Everyt'ing was so fine. His sisters, Bessie and Tessie, bustled around making t'ings 'just so'. And Freddie's mother talked nice to me. Then she went into de bedroom. De food was elegant: chicken, soaked in wine; and riced potatoes and peas from de garden, with rolls and lots of butter in everyt'ing, and apple pie with cream.

De sisters hadn't forgotten a t'ing. Dey pushed my chair up against Freddie's until you couldn't have slid a piece of paper between dem, as if dis would convince me I couldn't get along in dis world without Fred, dat I should give my very self to him. "

Stephanie spoke up: "How did you get so far into this relationship without letting him know you weren't going the whole nine yards, Grandma? Sounds like he was quite a catch."

"Ach, you know, I liked to dance, and didn't want to miss out on de fun. I was just having a good time. It was a boy-girl t'ing dat got out of hand before I knew what was happening."

"Why couldn't you marry him? Sounds like he was fun!"

"He was fun all right, dancing all night; and fried chicken dinners outside on a blanket! Ach, himmel!" *("Oh, heavens!")*

"So why did you have to hold him at arm's length?"

"Well, I was just getting to dat, why I couldn't marry him. His home was cozy with doilies under glass hanging on de wall. They read: 'Home Sweet Home' and 'Home is Where de Heart is'. Doilies on arms of de overstuffed furniture, and fat plump pillows on de couch with pink and black covers, really pretty.

When I went dere I felt right at home. Bessie, de chunky sister who did de talking, offered me a glass of homemade rhubarb wine in a pink-stemmed glass, it was. I didn't know what to t'ink. But Papa had given me wine at home once. So I took a sip and found dat I loved it! Upon taking another sip de whole room suddenly seemed rosier!

Fred's eyes were riveted on me! He looked me up and down, especially on my bosom! At de time I t'ought it was ample, but it became lots larger after my babies came along.

Freddie and his sisters had set de trap, and I was dere lady!" She looked away for a second. "Now he pulled me real close. I t'ought it was too much. I wanted to t'ank him for de romantic dinner but didn't like his hungry eyes, and his hands around my neck so tight, with Bessie and Tessie standing right dere. I felt like I was being suffocated, and noticed de sisters looked down at de floor.

Dere house was so pretty with tiny yellow flowers in de wallpaper. A vase of daisies sat in de middle of de table. Tessie, de tall sister, lit de white candles. Den de sisters disappeared. Dat was Fred's cue, I guess. I remember de phonograph playing softly, and he seated me at de table. Den he poured me another glass of de intoxicating wine." She laughed in spite of herself. "Den out of his pocket he fished a beaudiful emerald ring.

Now Freddie knelt down on one knee. Like de honorable man he was, he asked me to marry him! I t'ink he had been waiting for dis moment a long time.

But I had to 'turn him down' because dis man had one flaw. My dear dancing Freddie was cross-eyed, and I was afraid if I married him I'd have cross-eyed kids!" (Makes sense to me.)

"Well, dat isn't de end of de story. Freddie wanted me so dearly dat he went *'under de knife' to have his eyes uncrossed, and died on de operating table!"*

Every word of this Freddie story is absolutely true, Reader/friend. -- Now my Mom thought about her first love some seventy odd-years after the fact. It was a touching scene. Her pent-up emotions gave way as she recalled how it was when she was an untouched maiden of twenty-one. She looked away.

"Maybe I should have married Freddie;" she began again. "I don't know. Years later he still came to my mind now and den, and what my life would'a been if I had taken de other path in life. De path dat led into Fred's arms, his heart, his nimble feet, and his crossed but gentle eyes. He truly was one-of-a-kind. I was so fond of him but I couldn't take dat risk. I have always wondered just how many babies I would have had with him." Be that as it may, she could never go back. Now in her later years she had time to ponder that fateful decision.

Anna sniffled again, then excused herself. These were bitter-sweet memories. This man who loved to dance and made her laugh would always be a question pussyfooting around in the back of her mind. "At de time I even wondered if God would forgive me," my mother admitted. She felt she was indirectly the cause of Fred's death. Actually, it was nobody's "fault". It was one of those things that just happened, like "no fault divorce". No one was to blame, but my mom didn't see it that way.

"I told myself I had to go on, no matter what kind of a hand life had dealt. I wasn't sleeping well after dat, and when I did sleep my dreams were a mix of dancing with Freddie and looking into his crossed eyes."

"What kind of work did Freddie do?" I asked, thinking talking a different subject might make her feel better.

"Ach, I t'ink he was a farmer. Jah, dat was it. Dey had a little farm by Parkers Prairie. I can't remember much about dat and anyone living at dat time has long ago passed on. I guess I've outlived dem all."

Anyone would be hard-put to imagine a worse tragedy to befall our lovely innocent Anna. She now carried a heavy burden of guilt. "I cried until my eyes were swollen, turning it over and over in my mind." (And if a good man was as scarce then as now no doubt she had cause to worry!) "Never again would I see Freddie dancing his cares away. I told myself I was selfish to want so much." She twisted her handkerchief harder. "But everybody told me I was not to blame."

My mother cleared her throat, smiling as if to someone in her dreams, moisture in her eyes. "I t'ought about Freddie's mother, and Bessie and Tessie. He wouldn't be seated at their table again. I took full responsibility for Fred's untimely death, and like dat." Those were dark days indeed for her.

"Only God knew what anguish Mama Zinter and Freddie's sisters endured at the death of dere son and brother. Freddie's mother had always been satisfied with Fred's eyes. She couldn't believe I found dem distracting.

Not a t'ing could I do to rectify matters either. I walked the path to Freddie's house bawling all de while. De path seemed twice as long. I worried about what Mother Zinter would say.

Freddie had been de love of my life, crossed-eyes and all. Now when I went dere de adages on de wall didn't shine and look happy anymore. De brown overstuffed furniture looked tattered and worn.

Mama Zinter made herself scarce when I visited dere after dat. She didn't have a sentence to say to me. And who could blame her? She, who had hoped to become my mudder-in-law.

De sisters and I talked about Freddie and what a good person he was, but nobody broached the subject of Fred's eyes. Dat would have been too much.

Now -- between jobs -- I became despondent, not able to shake de guilt, spending weeks in my room. Mama worried about me. She said de house felt like a tomb. I wasn't speaking to anyone unless necessary and then only *'jah'* or no. I didn't even go to church. Mama begged me to go, but I couldn't leave my room. Mama said dat when she came upstairs to check on me I hadn't combed my hair in weeks. I was up dere living in a world of depression. Mama brought meals up to me, but I never went downstairs. I remember she brought me bread pieces soaked in warm milk many times, with a little sugar and cinnamon. I ate a little, but never had much of an 'appetize'."

In Anna's more rational hours she said she wondered if she would ever again enjoy dancing with another man. People stopped in after church to see her. They spoke kindly, offering condolences. She was appreciative, to be sure. Nevertheless, Fred's death left an empty space in her heart that could never be assuaged, leaving her with only sad memories. "What worried me de most was dat I might not find anybody I could like as much as Freddie."

CHAPTER III "I THEE WED"

So when the swashbuckling Edgar M. Rosenburg, my father, arrived at her doorstep looking for a hired girl Anna didn't think it over too long. She emerged from her room like a wounded butterfly coming out of its cocoon. She splashed icy-cold water from the water pitcher into her eyes, and hurriedly brushed her hair as best she could. Then she deliberately took one step and then another down the steep stairway to speak to this prospective employer. She felt this job migiht be just what she needed for her heart to heal. She had heard of Sleepy Eye, and knew a job should keep her mind occupied and be good therapy for her wounded soul.

"It had taken me quite long to get used to dis new life, employed on de Rosenburg Ranch, longer den it should have to learn de names of de children, but Mr. Rosenburg had not noticed. I couldn't talk naturally to de children, but I took it a day at a time. Gradually de scary dreams went away. Edgar's little girls made me smile, and slowly I came out of my shell.

Wild chokecherry trees grew all over. Somebody had planted a row of dem along de driveway. De berries were much too sour to eat out of hand. But mama and us girls had 'canned' even before I started 'working out' and in de fall I used dem to make wonderful chokecherry jelly.

My days were busy, with not a moment to t'ink about Fred during de day. Nights were different. I wrote long letters to mama and papa but before finishing de pages were tear-stained. I let dem lay on de dresser overnight to dry out before putting in de envelope. I remember sticking a one and a half-cent stamp on de letters. Sometimes I sent de folks a picture postcard. Dese needed only a penny stamp, or was it a half-penny, I forget now.

It would take a long time before I got back to my old routine. I brushed my hair a hundred strokes before bed again. Den I puttered around straightening drawers until I blew out de lamp.

De rooms upstairs at de ranch had two iron double beds. De girls shared one room. Albert had another room and I had my room, a smaller room with only one double bed. Sometimes Helen or Hildie slept with me. "Dad" had de downstairs bedroom just off de parlor. And like dat.

But sleep didn't come easy. My poor tortured body tossed around like a little boat in de stormy sea til finally I drifted off. My feather-pillow was damp and heavy by morning. It would be months before I would 'get over' my Freddie. In my dreams I saw him on de operating table, a dim bulb overhead.

I really liked children and was glad to see de girls clowning around. They seemed to be everywhere, playing in de haymow down at de barn and practicing somersaults and handstands in de grass. Dey were good girls and never gave me any trouble. I wondered if dey might call me 'Mother' some day.

Morning and evening Martha and Selma helped Albert with chores outside while Johanna helped me prepare meals. It was a warm happy way to go and I was feeling better. I tried to have supper ready when Dad and Albert got t'rough milking in de evening. Dad would go to work at de creamery in town but dat was not until years later.

One sunny afternoon Johanna stood at de stove washing dishes. She had removed a lid from de stove, and placed de metal dishpan directly over de flame on de wood range to keep her sudsy water warm. I kept a glimmer of fire going in de stove all day even in summer. De girls scalded de dishes with boiling water from de teakettle, so they were clean and germ-free.

Den Marty and Selma wiped de dishes with flour-sack towels, putting dem away in de pantry. Dere dey hung de old metal colander, egg-beater, wooden potato-masher and soup ladle. De dishes were heavy so if dey dropped one it didn't break, only chipped. And de glasses were heavy too, but sometimes dey broke into a t'ousand pieces. Den de girls grabbed de broom and dustpan and swept up de glass. Clara had taught dem well. And dey didn't squabble or get bossy either. Dey worked together as a team. Sometimes I heard de snap of dishtowels as dey wiped de dishes. De girls were feeling better after dere mother's death.

De spacious kitchen had a pleasing, comfortable feeling. Varnished dark wainscoting came halfway up de wall. Above dat it had been painted yellow. Scuff marks showed by de woodbox where Albert dropped an armload of firewood. I kept t'inking de walls needed a fresh coat of paint, but with so much to do I didn't say anyt'ing to Mr. Rosenburg about it.

Red-hot coals falling from de cook stove had burnt messy, black holes in de linoleum. Just behind de wall with de stove was a walk-in pantry. We could walk in one end, go t'rough de pantry and out de other end, very convenient. De girls helped me wash clothes and we had starched de pale-green organdy curtains. A kerosene lamp sat high in a bracket on de woodwork over de door leading to de upstairs. Another lamp sat on top of de wood range. When de dishes were done and de floor was swept de room looked really friendly.

A few days after arriving at de ranch I suggested to de girls dat we take a walk down around de farm. Dey were finishing up de dishes after dinner. Jo took another swipe with her dishrag along de back of de stove, wiping up crumbs until de rag was steaming. Den she hung it on a hook in de pantry.

We walked along a field and a little woods, de girls showing me dis and dat, where nettles grew and looking for poison ivy. De girls found wild daisies and picked dose. Dere fingers were yellow with daisy-dust before we got back to de house.

When Edgar and Albert worked in de fields de girls and I carried sandwiches, cake and a t'ermos of hot coffee to de men in mid-afternoon. We pushed down de fence to get to where dey were cultivatin' corn." There the eight of them enjoyed their afternoon break and the lovely banter that brothers and sisters pass back and forth in a healthy family.

"On de return to de house de girls picked wild roses and daisies growing by de stone pile, snacking on de tiny, wild strawberries dere. Hildie had to be watched closely as dere was a snarl of rusty barbwire in and among de rocks. It was a happy carefree time for de girls. Dey still mourned dere mother so were glad to go on dese trips to de fields.

As I picked de fragile roses my fantasy had them floating all de way to heaven. Fred reached out to dem. Now he's running t'rough wild roses in slow motion. My vision had him healt'y and strong. He turned to look at me and smiled. His look was pure passion. Suddenly I heard a shrill scream!

De scream brought me back to de real world. Little Hildie had stepped barefoot on a zigzagging green garter snake, a foot long. I picked up de little girl, telling her dose little snakes are just as afraid of her as she was afraid of dem, dat she mustn't cry." The garter snake didn't know what all the commotion was about. He never intended any harm. He was just passing through.

"Den our little troop headed home; we had had enough excitement for one day. Sally arranged de wildflowers putting dem in 'water tumblers'. Hildie put a vase of de wild roses in every room of de house. De scent was heavenly."

Here was Anna thrust into the role of not-only hired girl and housekeeper, but also nurse, counselor, governess, teacher, chef. The list went on and on. She tried hard and it made her feel good to be surrogate mother to this family. The job was immeasurably different from working for the Dr. Penney's, but it wasn't long before she felt right at home in the big old rambling farmhouse.

"I had learned a lot about meal-planning in my job at de Pennys. Here on Chokecherry Lane I put my knowledge about eating de right foods into practice, making sure meals were well-balanced. De girls helped and dey waxed healt'y and strong, like a well-watered garden. I used fruit in dessert when dat was possible during de long winters, serving plenty of fresh vegetables in summer. I loved to can so had lots of canned fruit and berries from de cellar on dose dreary days of winter. I liked to cook; it was a fun t'ing for me. And like dat.

Johannah was another right hand. She went ahead peeling potatoes before meals and washing dishes after meals. She was my assistant in everyt'ing inside de house. Jo was always quick to come 'across' to help." Anna and Jo had had a good rapport.

"Marty and Selma did de upstairs work and helped Albert and Dad outside with chores. Helen was like a shadow over little Hildie. De girls all had a job. Helen enjoyed mothering her little sister; and took her job seriously. De two girls played by demselves, and sometimes brought me dandelions or hollyhocks. Dat was nice."

Reader/friend, I think Anna told me a lot of things she never divulged to anyone else, perhaps because I had married a hometown boy. She liked him ever so much.

"Helen and Hildie were growing up fast since dere mother's death." Anna says. "De older girls read fairy-tales to dem before bedtime. Dad had brought home a new jump rope, and dey were putting dat to good use. And dey played hopscotch in de gravel in de yard.

I didn't try to hug dem too much because dey were used to being mothered by Johanna, Mart'a and Selma. Helen showed Hildie how to set table. Every one of de girls pulled on de rope of life together. Life was good.

At dis time in my life Freddie was becoming only a memory. De gloomy t'oughts I once had were being replaced with happy days."

Her depression had lifted and she was feeling like her old self again. My mom took another sip of her beloved coffee. "Now when I got up in de morning I looked forward to de new day! I gave t'anks to God every morning for dis new life. I told myself I would look for de good t'ings in my life every day!"

Parkers Prairie and Sleepy Eye are in the heart of the Bible Belt. The people have a deep devotion to God and it shows in their love for each other. When church bells toll on Sunday folks can be seen streaming from their lodgings on frosty mornings in winter and shirtsleeve days of summer. The scene reminds me of a Grandma Moses painting, with the chilluns, and grownups running off to church, cats and dogs friskying along.

Now, when Mr. Rosenburg, Anna, and the family marched into church on Sunday heads turned this way and that. The church-people wanted to get a glimpse of Edgar's new house-keeper. They couldn't help but notice how pretty she was and how erect she walked. She had a regal quality about her carriage. The ladies came up to her and talked just to see what she had to say. And she didn't disappoint them. She had never been quiet, but as a young lady she may have been just the slightest bit reticent.

Albert helped his dad care for the animals. He was the image of his dad even as a boy. He walked like Dad, talked like him, and tilted his cap like him. Actually, Dad didn't wear caps; he wore hats. But if he had, Albert would have done it the same. It was downright spooky. The older Albert became, even into his sixties, the more he grew into his father's image.

Anna continued: "I had been brought into de house purely as a 'hired girl.' Dad had had no other motive at dat time. Now suddenly *he began to notice me!* It was a Saturday afternoon. De girls and I had gone down to de hayfield when I caught him staring at me! He and Albert were making these cute little haystacks. I recall de day as if it were yesterday! I had worn a sky-blue polka dot dress with matching ribbon in my hair.

As de wind began to blow, my dress swelled out with de breeze. Bending over to pick de wild strawberries, again I caught him staring! He looked away but somet'ing told me he was interested. I had given him only a fleeting glance. I t'ought he was handsome when we first met, but I had been mourning for Freddie at dat time."

Edgar and Anna had lost their respective darlings at much the same time so it was only natural that they would have been attracted to each other. Indeed, it would have seemed a bit strange had they not. At any rate Anna told Steph and me it was another Saturday that summer that Edgar made his first move. A nasty wind was howling out of the North and it looked like rain. Anna had sent Sally out to check on Helen and Hildie. It was 10 o'clock and Anna had not seen them since breakfast.

"Den I set to work baking cinnamon rolls. Dat morning I mixed de dough and let it raise. After rolling it out I sprinkled on cinnamon/sugar. My hair was moist with perspiration, and wispy curls hung down around my face. De kitchen was humming with activity, the teakettle whistling, steam bubbling up t'rough de spout. Suddenly I realized somebody was standing at de kitchen door. I looked up; dere stood your Grandfather! It was one of de few times in my life dat I was at a loss for words! He made a pretense of looking for Albert, and asked me if I had seen him.

He smiled and I did a full blush, red blood consuming my face and entire neck area. I could feel my neck getting hot. Unable to speak I stared at him, slowly shaking my head back and forth."

The two of them were transfixed, staring at each other for a matter of minutes. Now some seventy years later Anna told us she had never seen eyes as blue as Edgar's. He later told her he had seen a halo around her hair, cast by the kerosene lamp. Love was beginning to blossom.....

"Quickly putting de rolls to raise I looked in de mirror above de washstand. Dere was flour on my cheek and forehead, where I had pushed my hair back. I wondered whether he had noticed my high cheekbones. Grabbing a brush I gave my hair a quick run-t'rough. I ran upstairs and found a decorative tortoise-shell comb, a gift from Freddie. Putting it in my hair I told myself I mustn't wear it down to de fields.

One day I realized I'd been cooking Edgar's favorite foods. He 'specially liked pork chops and sauerkraut with applesauce on de side. And I was t'inking more about my grooming, picking out just de right dress and sweater for any given day."

"Den dere was de time Ed was wanted on de phone. I went outside looking for him, finding him down in de machine shed, soldering somet'ing. Edgar said de phone could wait. He had more important t'ings to do. With dat he t'rew me across his arm, bent down and kissed me hard on de mouth! -- It felt good to have a man's arms around me again. -- Den he traced the hairline of my forehead with two fingers." She allowed herself a little laugh. "De phone was left dangling.....

Mulling dis newfound attention over at night I hardly knew how to act around 'Ed'. My previous beau had seemed more like a kitten compared to dis *'He-man.'"*

My Dad's favorite expression had been: "Women are hard to figure," so I think he was totally unprepared for Anna's coquettish glances. Quickly Anna went on, as if not told now she may never recall it again.

"I t'ink he liked de way his children were accepting me. Dey liked to imitate de way I talked. I smiled at dat."

When she first arrived at Chokecherry Lane my mother told me she had sat down at mealtime. She had not been eating regularly and her weight was down, but after she reached her normal weight she sampled the food while cooking and didn't have much of an "appetize" after that. She would rather wait on the youngsters and Edgar. She served a lot of pork, also beef roast, beef "patties" and vegetable soup.

And she served her own tasty home-baked bread. She liked to bake bread and always used her own sourdough starter.

"So when 'Dad' proposed marriage I looked at him one more time, checked to see dat his eyes worked together, and happily consented to be his bride." My mom blinked a few times, and untangled her hankie. She went on: "Dat night after Ed proposed when I slipped in between de sheets my mind was all a-twitter. No use trying to sleep, I wanted to ponder dis proposal for awhile. Being a wife was a 'step-up' from being merely a housekeeper. There wouldn't be a speck more work to do, but t'ink of all the advantages! And I wouldn't miss de nightlife.

Dat was all in de past buried with Freddie. But dere would be visits to Aunt Lucy and Uncle Fred, also "Tante" (Aunt) Lena,

Clara's sister. And my sisters, Ida, Emma and Louise, besides my brothers Walter, Louie and dere wives. And Dad took me to visit Mama and Papa. Dat was what we did for fun. I knew I'd miss de money coming in, but liked de idea of people calling me 'Mrs. Rosenburg.' I would get along fine.

My chances of meeting someone else were not good. I didn't get off de farm except for school programs, and hadn't seen anyone interesting at church.

Now I looked forward to sleeping in de four-poster bed in de downstairs bedroom..... And what could be more fun den moving from de upstairs to de downstairs!"

So with all due respect to her first love my Mom made plans to marry Mr. Edgar Martin Rosenburg. From the moment Anna accepted Edgar's proposal she said she had moved through time as if living a fairy-like existence, practically floating above the ground. Here was a man who clearly loved her. And God knows he needed her. The girls were lovely little girls, but they needed a mother-figure in their lives, a confidante to smooth out the stoniness in their daily lives.

She loved the wide expanse of farmland. Here she could rub the rich Minnesota soil between her toes. The growing season was short, but when the farmer planted his grain and veggies something akin to an explosion occurred as the tender plants shot forth from the ground. Summers became hothouses, the air so humid. But that was the price people paid to live in this pristine portion of God's resplendent "Land O Lakes." Anna had always liked Minnesota; the loamy soil was much like that of her native Germany.

"I laid awake far into de night after Edgar's proposal. I wondered how he was sleeping, whether he slept as well since his first wife died. I, myself, couldn't find de right position for sleep. When first coming to de ranch I was fraught with sad t'oughts of Freddie. Now I laid awake t'inking about Edgar. Sometimes I wondered if I really did love him or if I only felt sorry for him. But dis warm feeling came all over my body when he looked at me, so I felt it was true love. And he always greeted me politely in de morning, so no matter whether I had slept or not I gave him my best smile. I noticed he looked up into my face when I waited on de table, setting out de food. I liked dat.

I laid awake t'inking about de master bedroom. I didn't want it too frilly, maybe a pretty dresser-scarf, something with cupids, putting my husband in just de right mood for making love..... I t'ought about new curtains in dere. As de new wife I felt I could have a few ideas dat were my very own.

I'd found a splendid husband and togedder we would make beaudiful music. We had not talked about making babies, but I wanted a large family. Now during my engagement I t'ought about dat. Maybe seven or eight babies would be nice, about half girls and half boys; dat was how I figured it." (She would make her mark on the world!)

The daughters liked the idea of their father's betrothal. When Anna asked one of the little *"heartzen"* (hearts) to do an errand, she fairly flew to do Anna's bidding. Even the seasoned Edgar was caught up in the excitement. He was seen shining the bridles for his steeds, and Sally had heard him softly humming while currying the horses. A feeling of romance was in the air...

Anna described her wedding day in her heavy German accent. "Even Freddie's Mudder and sisters showed up at my wedding to dis new man. Dey had cried long enough. I s'pose dis was Mrs. Zinter's way of telling me I shouldn't blame myself for de way t'ings turned out. It made me feel so good. De little cat'edral was called *De Spires*. Four spires besides de steeple, dere was."

It was a happier occasion for our hard-working Anna. Now my Mother took Steph and me into the bedroom where her wedding picture hung above the headboard of the four-poster bed. It was in a large oval frame, fashionable at the time. My mother looks elegant standing next to dad, who is seated. Both are stiff as cardboard cutouts. Anna looks almost sad on that day of days, her lips clamped together, as if she had bitten into a pickle, put up with too much vinegar. Dad, dressed in a single-breasted brown suit looks stern. Those expressions may have been the style in the winter of 1914……

Anna wore an ivory gown, headdress and train. Her veil was finger-tip length with rows of ruffles in her gown. Her long sleeves came to a point over her strong hands.

"I had been very tired on my wedding day," she explained, "but told myself I'd get back to normal in a few short days. Dat little cathedral was so pretty, painted entirely white on de outside. It was mid-winter, December t'irty. Friends and family on both sides traveled long distances for the afternoon occasion. Coffee, tea and cake was all de relatives needed. After de reception friends left for de long trip back to dere homes. Even de weather had cooperated. It was hovering around t'irty degrees if my memory is correct. De ladies wrapped up in furry lap robes and muffs for de trip home in de buggies."

I, Rudy, have a hard time understanding why Edgar's little *"heartzen"* didn't attend the wedding. Perhaps that was the custom at the time. It seemed like an era when children were second-class citizens, at least in the Rosenburg household. But don't get me started on that, Reader/friend. That's a sore subject with me.

"On de return to de Ranch after my wedding I was really miffed," Anna said firmly, her eyes darkening. "I had been given a place in de back seat of de buggy while a 'gentleman' of doubtful character rode up front with Edgar!"

She was only mildly angry at the time. Now, in the eighties, with Women's Lib so real, she did indeed feel this was wrong, very wrong. Perhaps Edgar thought his bride would be warmer in the buggy; I think that was it. It makes me wonder if it ever crossed Anna's mind that this might be a sign of things to come in their marriage.

My mom told me that some of the church ladies thought she was "stuck up" because she held her head so high when she walked into church with the family, but that was just something she did naturally. We have pictures of her when she was single. Her dark hair came over her ears in lovely waves. My Mom did have a prominent wart on one side of her nose, but after a person got to know her it was never noticed. Her facial features were quite lovely.

In her "later years" Anna told me Dad had scolded her for spending so much money on her wedding gown. Perhaps that explains her expression in the portrait. But he had also said: *"You're worth your weight in gold. You're worth your weight in gold'......"* I can't help but wonder how much time elapsed before he stopped uttering those words. Whatever the case, I learned that this union had been a volatile relationship early on.

It causes me to wonder how much money Dad spent on her. He must have held her romantically, sidling up to her while she was cooking, stealing a kiss. But I wonder if he ever brought her flowers or "puferme." I had always held my Dad in such high esteem. Now he was emerging in a slightly different light. Dad was definitely a chauvinist, but who could blame him. I mean, chauvinism was the "in" thing at the time.

To her marriage Anna brought a lovely piece of furniture for her dowry as this was a tradition from the Old Country. She chose a beautiful oak desk. Antique dealers might say this was a “secretary”, but all the secretaries I've known sat down and typed. This one didn't; therefore it must have been a desk. As we grew up Anna placed our confirmation pictures in the desk. Then when we were grown and came home on holiday we could see how we looked when we were young and gay.

Anna speaks: "De ladies in de community seemed to t'ink I was a lucky woman to have six 'built-in' babysitters when we married. Others said I was de babysitter to six kids; you know how women like to talk, but I didn't care. If dey wanted to talk and it made dem feel better, let dem talk!"

Personally, I thought it was half-and-half. Nevertheless, Anna was a young lady of twenty-three. She had to “rule and govern” (her words) this large family day in and day out with never a day off for holidays. That ought to sober up the most frivolous bride. I had to give my Mom a lot of credit.

She always did wash and clean until everything had a happy homey countenance. "But," my Mom now said happily: "since marrying ‘Ed’ it seemed like more fun! De girls were doing dere part and I was depending on dem more and more."

Anna told me that she surely loved her husband, but she began to notice a certain friction in her marriage after the first few weeks they were hitched. Nevertheless, she was now married and would do her best to make it work. All the frivolities of the past were gone. They had their differences to be sure, but she would carry the torch onward with every fiber of her being for this man and his ready-made family.

If Anna approached the marriage bed with the same gusto as in her daytime endeavors she must have been a tigress in bed.

Whatever the case, her firstborn Edgar begat arrived *eleven months* after they tied the marriage bond. And can you guess what she named this new little son? *She named him Fred!* Anna had a brother by that name, so whether she named him after her brother or her long lost lover no one knew. Edgar was so thrilled to have another son he couldn't have given a crock what she named the baby. He had agreed with Anna, to name her firstborn Fred, and no doubt he did want to please his bride.

"I remember when Fritzie was born." said Anna, smiling. "He was born at home, as were all my babies. I had never felt so fulfilled. Being a mudder was what I had dreamed about, 'specially now since Freddie died. Dis was what life was all about. I counted de little fingers and toes. He was perfect, and I remember Dad saying: 'He has your brown eyes.'"

It had not been a difficult delivery. I'd always been active, and I t'ink dat made de difference. And I was slender; I t'ink dat helped. My labor was not so bad, and nobody tried to scare me, as I'd heard from de old wives' tales. Labor was only dat, hard work. From dat time on I never had a qualm about delivery. With Dr. Will being so near, right dere in Sleepy Eye I wasn't a bit afraid of what de future held." She was a pioneer of sorts.

"I surely enjoyed my firstborn, showering him with kisses and every kindness. He was a beautiful baby. At ten months he walked, I remember. My dreams were being played out day by day and I had never been happier. De girls couldn't hardly keep dere hands off dis precious little manchild. Helen and Hildie loved to hear me sing him lullabies. I let dem hold de baby as long as dey sat down. Dey liked to play 'patty-cake' with de baby. Den I nursed him; dey loved to watch dat. After nursing I rocked little Fritzie and sang him to sleep."

I (Rudy) never remembered Fred living at home. He had left home when he was about 19. My older brothers and sisters seemed more like aunts and uncles than siblings. My sisters said Fritz had been a whistler. When somebody looked for him they listened for his whistle, and they could usually find him.

Anna continued her story: "About two years after Fritz was born I guess I was t'inking all de right t'oughts when along came another bonny baby boy! Carl Bernhardt Wilhelm looked more like Dad's side of de family, with blue eyes and tan hair."

("Well," Edgar may have thought. "This woman knows what it's all about! She has given me two sons. Perhaps she'll give me two more!") What joy there was in the Rosenberg household with the addition of Anna's second son! "This is great!" said Edgar in his stage whisper. "Now I have three sons to help me work and tame the land!"

My Mom must have heard the stage whisper because it wasn't long before she was "that way" again. She rather enjoyed being pregnant. I think she felt sex was a God-given pleasure for her husband and she would go along with it. When she carried a baby in her belly her complexion took on a lovely glow. Anna was not a big eater and didn't gain an ounce normally, but when pregnant her appetite peaked, and she would "fill out."

(Decades later when I became a mother Anna told me she nursed her babies as long as she could because as long as she was nursing she didn't become pregnant. There's food for thought there. However, I was never successful in nursing my babies, so was not able to determine whether her theory worked or not.) My babies came fast and furious, including a set of twins. But Anna's babies came down the lane in single file every two years like clockwork.

Going back to the lineage the third child Anna bore, a girl, was named Sidonia. This baby was blessed with silky blonde hair and was an unusually fair child with fine features. Sid worked hard as did all the sisters. And this sister was a reader. In the evenings Sid could always be found in a quiet corner of the parlor with her nose in a book.

These nine offspring were so much fun there was no stopping them now. At any rate Sid's birth began a string of girls.

Next in line was a brunette, Clara, named after Dad's first wife. "Clarie" was the tallest of the girls, five foot, nine. And she walked tall, not stooped over. I remember her best for her delightful sense of humor.

After Clara the inimitable Francesca -- nicknamed Frankie -- made her debut. Like Clara she graduated eighth grade and worked on the farm before going down to the "twin cities," Minneapolis and St. Paul. She was knownfor her lusty laughter.

The next member of the family, Esther, picked up the baton, and with smiling eyes said: "Let the party begin!" When there was a significant event in the family such as a birth or death, a baptism or wedding Esther managed to be there, or at least the first one of the siblings on the scene. *And* she did much to pave the path to high school.

In due time God gave Anna and Edgar another boy. This was Roland - nicknamed Rosie. This baby was born two years after Esther, almost to the day. A handsome lad, he was, even as a small boy. And he was tall and muscular. As he grew Roland delighted in tantalizing us girls. He liked his placement in this clan, sandwiched in the midst of a dozen females. Dad's happiness knew no bounds as he welcomed this new little son.

Rosie was born in mid-April. Mom told me the snow was melting and "running off the eaves." That sounds like Rosie, throwing a party the day he was born! My Mother was glad to deliver another son. This new son would please her husband, and make life more pleasant, at least for a while.

Not only was Rosie born that certain day in April, but also my Dad had begun his job as secretary of the Land O Lakes creamery in Sleepy Eye that very day. Albert, Fritz and Carl were getting big enough to take care of the ranch. Dad hired a man at some point in time but I don't know when that began.

I had seen the big book where dad entered the debits and credits. He had the most beautiful handwriting I had ever seen. It was truly remarkable. Handwriting was an art in those days.

Edgar made benches for his burgeoning family as it was the smart thing to do. As more and more babies came along, no problem, he just made longer and longer benches. If we had company at mealtime we kids scrunched together at the table making more room and more fun for everybody. Neighbors usually sat down to eat too. Most of the farmers did like that.

Dad's favorite motto had been: "There's always room for one more." This rule applied when riding in the car as well as at the table. If somebody needed a "lift" my Dad obliged even if we were packed as tightly in the car as little fishies in a flat can. One or two more people could always be squeezed in. That was common practice in those days.

There was the widow lady and her five-year-old son who walked to church on Sunday. She lived a half-mile out of town. Going home she and the little boy would get a head start on us and would be halfway there when we came along in the car. Our black Chevie was filled to the rafters with kids dangling from the windows, cheeks pressed against the glass; but Dad always picked up the lady and her child. He was driving perhaps thirty-five mph, and as the car slowed we piled on each other's laps making room for the pedestrians. My dad certainly practiced what he preached in that instance.

It makes me wonder if dad uttered those words "always room for one more" when Anna told him she was pregnant again. Or maybe she didn't tell him. I personally think she didn't. She no doubt figured he would find out in his own good time. Conversely, if she did tell him he must have retorted: "So what else is new!"

After Rosie, my sister Barbara arrived. Anna picks up the story: "De new baby was already ten days old and had not been named. We were at de school for de spring picnic. I was seated in a circle of mothers with dis new baby girl. De ladies were giving me all kinds of names for my new baby. Dey suggested names like: Freida, Eva, and Elsie, gently passing de baby around. Suddenly Edna Hofdahl, who was holding de baby announced: 'If you don't name dis baby Barbara I'm going to drop her!'

All right, it's Barbara" I said, laughing. "And dat was how it went. When Barbara was in grade school she was so smart de teacher let her skip a grade. She went directly from second to fourt' grade. Dis isn't done anymore, but it happened just dat way back in nineteen hundred, and t'irty-five. And like dat."

Next in line, the star of the show, that's me Rudy. I'm number fifteen. Anna had taken a light-hearted approach to childbearing for years now. -- They named me after the Ruth in the Bible, and I've been trying to live up to that name ever since! Just a bit of humor for you there, Reader/friend.

Born in the dead of winter my mom said it was snowing hard and drifting that day. She and Inez, the hired girl, had wondered whether the doctor could get through but he had arrived just in the nick of time. He had gotten stuck by the cemetery and had to get out and shovel snow.

Inez Denow, the hired girl, had not been worried though, sure she could handle the delivery alone. She felt she knew as much as the midwives.

When I was little I had thin ash-blonde hair. It has gotten very thick over the years. Guess I inherited my thick hair from my Mom, also inherited her affinity for sketching. I've been sketching and oil painting all my life; Anna told me in her later years that she had had the same hobby as a young girl. -- And we all got our determination from her.

After me came my little sister Carrie. She was named after Dad's sister, Aunt Carrie. That was a fun event. This baby was a brown-eyed beauty who instantly captivated the entire clan. Born on the very day that Franklin Delano Roosevelt was elected to the presidency, dad -- a staunch Democrat -- could hardly contain himself. Passing out the customary cigars he was so elated he could have flown into work under his own power!

When the Sleepy Eye Herald, the weekly newspaper, came out a few days later the stork column read: *"A baby girl was born to Mr. and Mrs. Edgar M. Rosenburg on November 8, (1932). If the baby had been a boy no doubt he would have been christened 'Franklin Roosevelt Rosenburg.'"* -- Wouldn't that have been a mouthful! -- We all were secretly glad the baby was female, but nobody dared say so. I mean, my dad was the Supreme Commander of the Household! Nobody sassed my Dad. *Nobody!*

A couple years later Anna was nearly ready to call it quits. Not quite ready. She felt very relaxed as she delivered her final gift to the world: Edgar Michael Rosenburg, Jr., nicknamed Mickey. (Rootkin wondered if she had them all straight, and Rudy decided, yes that's correct.)

All of Anna's babies were born at home as this was the era of midwives. But Anna had had Dr. Will present at every one of her eleven deliveries.

I recall the first cry of child #17, Mickey. Not quite five I was standing quietly against the wall in the parlor taking it all in. The old house had a magical atmosphere. A new citizen was about to make his appearance on the world stage.

My mother's boudoir, the "birthing room" led off the parlor. Suddenly everything started happening at once! The hired girl, Inez, ran for a basin of boiling water and assisted Dr. Will as needed. I always wondered why the boiling water was so important, but now think it was needed to keep the doctor's instruments sterile. I must have taken a peek into the chamber because I remember seeing Inez putting long sterile stockings over my Mom's legs all the way up to her crotch. -- I was quickly shooed away and went to stand by the wall in the parlor again.

It wasn't long before I heard a robust wail. I wondered how many more babies would be born, but this was to be the last of the Rosenburg siblings. Everybody was glad that this last baby was a boy rounding out the family to a dozen girls and five boys.

Many years after Mickey was born Dr. W. W. Will was named "The Best in the U.S. among Country Doctors". This physician was certainly deserving of the title. -- He came out in all kinds of weather and always took a few minutes to chat with his patients. Greatly loved was he. It was a very small town where everybody knew the latest gossip and a secret could not be kept. But in a way it was nice because when there was trouble all these people could be praying for you.

The good doctor told Inez this had always been the nicest thing about his practice, delivering babies. As a child I wondered how they knew Mickey would be the last one, therefore naming him Junior.

Will never forget how my Mom diapered the baby. She sat down, placed the baby across her knees, grabbed a diaper pinning it on him. I've never seen anyone else do that, but it seemed to be second nature with her. Looking back on it I think it was the easiest and only way to go for her.

After Mickey's birth my Dad counted his children and realized he had produced a fine fettled family. It may not have been exactly what he would have wished for; he would have preferred more sons, but it was a fine family just the same. When he counted them he noted that he had seventeen children: five males and twelve females. And he did indeed appreciate every one of them whether he told them he loved them or not. He liked to call the kids, "the Gumps." I thought that was so cute.

My half-sister Selma (Sally) told me that when Anna was really busy, going in several directions at once, seemingly, she could be heard saying: "I'm busier than a baby between the layer cake!" That's pretty busy all right.

So with all these many progeny Anna felt like the mother to a gaggle of goslings. The hired girl helped with meals and cleaning, but didn't stay overnight since she lived just across the road. She was so much fun. When it thundered she told us kids that that was the angels up there bowling! We loved her. Her little girl, Donna, who was my age came along to our house too. That was all we needed, another sister! We did have more fun when Donna came along to play. It was an enchanting time for Carrie, Donna and me.

But Reader/friend, on this gigantic tribe thing, I'd like to make a comment. My dad had always been a devout churchgoer. I have an idea that when he opened his Bible and read right there in Genesis where God says: "Go ye therefore and multiply and tame the land", dad must have taken the Lord quite literally. Besides, any self-respecting farm family had to keep up with the Wickersteads down the road. And they had thirteen children!

My folks had acquired a captain's chair somewhere along the line. Dad used it as a disciplinary tool for my half-sisters and Albert. If one of the kids misbehaved he or she had to sit in "the chair." He never used the chair on us younger kids though. Guess he had given up on discipline by the time we came along. In my Mother's passion for painting she had swathered it with pink paint. It was still in the house when I was in high school.

Dad, in his love for politics would have liked to get into state government, but when he seriously considered it he felt he was getting too old. -- He had been a charter member of the Land O Lakes Corporation, and attended company meetings when I was a small child. I remember him being gone from home for days at a time, and have seen pictures of him as a charter member.

CHAPTER IV GERMANY TO AMERICA

My mother picks up her story. "Jah, I was born in Germany in 1891. When I crossed de ocean I was just t'ree years old. My brother, Fred, was seven and sister Ida was five at dat time.

Ida and I and brother Fred accompanied my mama, Dagmar, in coming to America. Papa was already here. He had gotten a job with de railroad; den sent for his family." Her voice lowered to a whisper. "Dere had been another brudder on board de ship, but he had drowned in de pee-pot!"

No doubt Dagmar, who would have been my grandmother, had she lived long enough, had plenty to grieve about at this difficult stage of her life but she bravely went on.

Dear Reader/friend: My Aunt Emma, born here in the States, did not have the strong accent my mother had. She gave me the following account of the story of their immigration, having heard the story from her mother and sisters many times: "After a month at sea they had been 'dumped off' (her words) on Ellis Island. There they were 'herded' to a certain area for new immigrants. On one of the tables some biscuits had been left. They were hungry, as they had not eaten. Mama picked up the biscuits putting them in a paper sack. She gave one to each of the children. They ate those, then looked around for more. She doled out one more each of them. Soon all the biscuits were gone, so they sat down and waited for Papa.

A man and his wife came by. Mama opened the sack to show that it was empty and she had no food for her children, but they shrugged their shoulders and went on. A little later another man passed by. Again Mama opened the empty sack; he trudged on also. They were so discouraged. I know Mama worried. Ida had said: 'The bench was hard, dark clouds loomed overhead and this new land was losing its luster.'

But," Aunt Emma went on: "Imagine their astonishment when a half-hour later the last man returned with a bag filled with rolls and doughnuts! How happy they were! Their faith in America had been restored. -- Some hours later Papa arrived at Ellis Island and the little family was back together once more. They took the train to the Midwest settling in Norwood, Minnesota. The rich loamy soil there was much like what they were used to in Germany.

The new location was not without hardship. Not speaking the language made it difficult, but we Germans are hardy folks. Papa and Mama persevered and soon met other new immigrants. It didn't take long before they were comfortable in their new home. The house they found was a neglected cabin; they were cramped, but could get by. Mama always made things 'homey' and my sister planted flowers around the house in the spring. Papa bought a spinning wheel and a table. They borrowed chairs from neighbors, and were 'making do.'

Mama attended the country school along with her children and took Anna along. -- She wanted to learn English and a lot more about this new adopted country. -- But the poor teacher had no time to work with Mama. She had forty-five pupils in one room here in the USA."

Reader/friend: Some years later I was on the phone talking to Aunt Louise, Anna's youngest sister. She told me the following story when she was eighty-eight years old and I am quoting her: "Once one of the boys didn't have his assignment done. The teacher beat him with a stick! Since our mama, Dagmar, had to leave school early in the afternoon to tend the sheep she wondered if she would also get a beating with a stick! Mama and Papa wondered if they had done the wrong thing in coming to this country. – I heard them say that Papa would stand at the head of the table, shake his head and murmur: 'This isn't as good as what we had!'"

Aunt Louise said there were eight grades in the one-room school. Ida, Fred, Mama and little Anna walked three-quarters of a mile. The girls wore leggings or long underwear under their handmade dresses the winters were so bitter cold. The customary lady teacher taught at the country school.

Tante (Aunt) Emma told me that the question had come up whether the teacher could teach in the German language. The law was passed that the teacher could not, a comforting thought to me.

My cousins in Miltona, near the larger town of Alexandria spoke only German until they began school. There they learned English right along with the 3-R's. They were bi-lingual. Not so with the Rosenburg kids. We were never lucky enough to learn German. The only time our parents spoke in their native tongue was when they didn't want us to know what they were saying. Knowing two languages was very convenient in that way.

Dad's people had immigrated from Richtenberg Deutschland settling in the Chicago area. Dad loved to tell us about Mrs. O'Leary's cow kicking over the lantern when she was milking, setting off the great Chicago fire, occurring in the latter part of the 1800's. It was one of the worst fires of the nineteenth century. Dad was born in 1876, a few years after the fire, but he had heard the story many times. He was a storyteller and told it well. Chicago was merely a fledgling city at that time.

Eventually my Rosenburg forefathers moved to Minnesota to the Sleepy Eye area. The Greskes had now moved from Norwood, settling in the little town of Parkers Prairie, not far from Lake Miltona. By this time they had several more children, and were contented members of the American Melting Pot.

The Edgar M. Rosenburg house was nice. A painting of Abraham Lincoln's birthplace hung in the parlor depicting a log cabin. The little lad Lincoln stands in the yard throwing grain to the chickens. The painting is truly gorgeous, done in the primitive style of the nineteen-tens.

An ornate clock sat high on a shelf gonging on the hour and the half-hour. It was wooden, rectangular, with curlicues around the edge and a pendulum swinging back and forth. The numbers on the clock were in Roman numerals. It was truly lovely.

An upright piano stood in the parlor like a silent member of the family. Many of the old farmhouses were like that. The piano occupied a prominent place in the parlor, more or less, just for looks. No one knew how to play it. To me, it seemed like a terrible waste, but that was then, and this is now.

On top of Anna's piano was a maroon and dark green velvet dresser-scarf fringed on the ends. And atop *that* was a gorgeous Christmas cactus. It burst into full bloom just in time for the holiday. The enormous plant fairly dripped with red and pink blossoms. I have fond memories of the big plant. Anna knew exactly what to do for the enormous plant to make it bloom at just the right time.

The buffet held lovely hand-painted platters, bowls and the genuine cut-glass water pitcher with matching bowl, gifts my folks had received when they were married, some from Dad's first marriage.

Anna rarely used her old treadle sewing machine. She did make doll dresses for the life-size dolls Carrie and I had gotten for Christmas one year. We had been given the big dolls, with buggies, when Carrie was three and I was almost five. The next

Christmas Mom made new dresses and slips for the dolls out of clothes my older sisters had cast off. We played with the big dolls so much that the original dresses had worn out in one year. Other than the doll dresses she didn't have time to sew as we grew_up. Her time was taken simply preparing meals and the thousand and one things that went on in that mammoth family.......

CHAPTER V ANNA & COMPANY

Once a week Anna's kitchen became a bakery as she turned out her home baked bread to feed this hungry crew. The only thing she lacked were those heavy-duty bread mixers. Loaves popped out of her oven like they were coming off an assembly line. It wasn't feeding the five thousand, but was close.

Saturday was bread-baking day. She fired up the wood stove, mixed the dough, kneading, punching and forming the loaves. When the bread had raised and nicely rounded off on top she put her wrist wa-ay back in the oven. Then she pulled her arm out. The oven wasn't hot enough. Anna put more wood in and fired her range up a little hotter. She put her arm in the oven a second time. When her wrist felt hot enough she popped the bread in!

She liked the wrist method of testing the oven temperature. That way she didn't need to rely on a thermometer, nor did she need to "hunt" around in a drawer for one. The hand and the wrist were always right there at the end of her arm! My mom made about fifteen loaves at a time, and was very protective of her bread, guarding it from drafts when Rosie brought in wood.

She had four or five bread pans, and each pan held three loaves of bread. Anna had always been frugal with her grocery money, trying to stretch her food dollar. She could have fed Afghanistan on twenty dollars a week!

In my reverie, Reader/friend, I see the little Rootkin (myself) on the stairs coming down for breakfast. The little girl, perhaps three, carries her socks and shoes in her hands. She makes a beeline to the commode to wash up using the metal basin, then takes her place on a bench at the humongous table.

The inviting aroma of bacon and maple syrup meets me all the way to the top of the stairs. Coming closer to the landing I smell grease burning off two black cast-iron skillets. Anna is making pancakes for this small army.

Our very own Anna who was once pursued so ardently now stands at the range dropping batter into the black frying pans. The "ding, ding, ding" of the large metal spoon slices the air as it hits the pan. It will take tall stacks of hotcakes to get this company of people filled up and on the move for the day.

We liked to put maple syrup on our hotcakes -- made from our own maple trees -- but more often we smeared on good old creamery butter and sprinkled on a little granulated sugar.

A well-worn green oilcloth covers the table. Anna leaves the stove long enough to slosh steaming coffee into the heavy white mugs. She does not look so elegant here. A brightly colored apron covers her faded housedress and it's apparent she has pinned her wispy hair away from her face in a hurry. Her brown lace-up shoes have a one-and-a-half inch heel. That's what she is most comfortable in. She wears mercerized stockings, heavy elephant wrinkles forming around her thin legs. Her appearance is not important to her. Her main thrust this morning is to get the multitude filled up and ready to meet the day.

The big table is occupied by big men. Roland sits there next to Dad. Carl's still there; also Gordon Larke and Martin Schmitz, the hired men. The men reach for the big box of corn flakes, filling cereal dishes. They scrunched the flakes real fine so they could be eaten faster I guess. (I don't know whether we had corn flakes and pancakes at the same meal, but I do remember the hired men scrunching up the corn flakes.)

Anna asked each of the men how many eggs he wanted. Roland, Carl and the hired men wolfed down five or six eggs for breakfast. They needed that kind of calories under their belts to keep their energy level up for the long workday.

We Rosenburgs were never ones to worry about calories, and if the word cholesterol had been coined we had not heard it.

Carl would not be there at the ranch much longer. He soon would follow Fred to Flint. I know at least one hired man was there because my mom always hid his cap for the Easter celebration. -- Am not sure whether the hired men were there during the worst part of the Great Depression. I was born in 1931, and am writing only what I observed.

Gordon Larke was a good friend of my brother Carl's. He had been born into a family so large they couldn't afford to feed them all during the Depression so Gordon worked on the Rosenburg Ranch to have a place to eat and sleep. I overheard my siblings say that he had not gotten paid.

Like my brother Carl, (lost in the Navy during World War II) Gordon also went to war and never came back. I don't know in which branch he served but I guess it doesn't really matter. Like they say: "War is Hell," and it doesn't matter whether you're on land, in the air or at sea.

When all these various-sized people had gathered 'round the immense table for a meal no one touched the food until Grace was offered. "Look, but don't touch," was the unwritten rule. We feasted our eyes on pork roast, mashed potatoes, and heavy china bowls of creamed carrots. My mom liked to cream things. It stretched the food and warded off hunger. We said prayers before breakfast, dinner and supper.

In retrospect I know the prayers before and after meals must have been a powerful witness for the Lord to the hired men and anyone who might be visiting. For dinner at noon Anna would have prepared chicken, roast pork or roast beef, or hamburger "patties." Vegetable soup (zuppa in German) or bean soup with ham hocks were also mainstays in our diet. When she didn't have her own home-baked bread for dinner she got busy and made biscuits. Fresh out of the oven, they were delicious!

Before meals the following prayer was offered:

"Come, Lord Jesus, be our guest.
And let these gifts to us be blessed. Amen."

And no one left the table before intoning:

"Our Lord we thank for meat and drink,
Through Jesus Christ, Amen."

After breakfast Rosie went out to fetch wood for the day. The woodbox stood just inside the kitchen door. He carried in the split wood, piled high against his chest, just so he could see over.

On Saturday while Anna baked, "the girls" did the cleaning. We were getting ready for Sunday. For supper on Saturday night we generally opened a large can or two of red salmon. This was put on a platter with raw Bermuda onion rings around the fish. The salmon and freshly baked bread with plenty of creamery butter was our supper. And it was good.

Anna was an ambitious soul. She loved to make pies for Sunday dinner. Rising early Sunday morning before anyone else was up -- perhaps 4:30 or 5 o'clock -- she made three or four pies whether company was coming or not. I can picture her rolling pin with the red handles, one partially broken off. "Pie-plant" pie was a favorite.

Carrie and I called it "pie-plant" pie too. Later I learned to call it "rhubarb." Early in the spring when the rhubarb was the sweetest Carrie and I went out to the garden, each of us carrying a half-cup of sugar. We broke off the rhubarb and dipped it in the sugar, eating it, pretending it was sugar cane. With enough granulated sugar, we thought it was good.

Anna also made a mean lemon pie, squeezing the lemons and piling on the meringue. We feasted on apple pie in summer, and pumpkin in the fall with everything made from scratch.

In the summertime my older sisters went up to northern Minnesota with dad and picked wild blueberries. They made it a three-day affair, driving up to the blueberry patch the first day, picking all afternoon, sleeping under the stars. They picked all day the second day; then picked in the forenoon on the third day, and dad driving home, the car smelling of blueberries. My half-sister Helen said she got so sick of picking the tiny wild berries she couldn't *look at another blueberry!*

Then we canned blueberries for days! I helped by picking them over, discarding green berries and tiny leaves. I had always wished I could go "up north" to pick berries, but by the time I was big enough we had moved into Sleepy Eye. Dad was too old and tired and the family had shrunk so this wasn't done any more. Guess I hadn't missed anything after all. Those wild blueberries are so small it would take hours to pick a small pail full.

In those bygone days of yesteryear there was no electricity in the rural areas. It may have been the norm in Sleepy Eye, but not in the country. However, we got along very well with kerosene lamps and "sad irons." The old table radio, powered by an automobile battery, brought us the news and our entertainment.

I can "see" my dad sitting in his "easy chair" listening to President Franklin D. Roosevelt as he delivered one of his famous "fireside chats." -- Can almost smell the tobacco in dad's pipe, the smoke ascending in neat little curls. In my mind's "ear" I hear the distinctive voice of FDR. He says "again and again and again," giving the second syllable the long 'a'. How I loved to hear the president talk. I think the whole country did!

Anna came into the front room to listen to the president for a few minutes. She loved to hear Roosevelt speaking over the "talking box." Then back she went to the kitchen. In those days she still didn't sit down at mealtime. The only time she sat down to eat was when we had company. But how she loved her coffee, drinking it hot, cold, or any stage in between. That's the way I am now. I guess it's true: "like Mother, like Daughter."

"Tell me more about your life back in those days, Gramma," the days before you had electricity," urged Stephanie.

"Well, let's see." Anna cleared her throat and began: "Once a week it was Rootie and Carrie's job to wash chimneys for de kerosene lamps. One lamp in de kitchen was perched high in a bracket on de woodwork. It had a round reflector behind it."

Reader/friend, I look back on that time quite fondly, perhaps because of its simplicity. And what defies explanation was how we kids walked up and down stairs - and all over the house - with the kerosene lamps and no one had an accident. The Lord was certainly watching over us. *And I remember being careful,* walking as if I had a book on my head.

Thinking about the kerosene lamps reminds me of the "curling iron" Barbie and I used. We hung the iron in the lamp chimney. When it was heated sufficiently we touched up our locks around the face a bit, looking like we had just stepped out of a salon, a dandy way to go. These have come back, but are electric now.

Ironing was a job we did religiously once a week. Barbie and I took turns with the old "sad" irons, those found in antique stores now. Pleasant memories of a different era and a slower pace come to me when I see Anna's sad irons in my home today.

Barbie and I ironed all day using the sad irons from the wood range. The kitchen smelled like a laundry as we removed the moisture from the clothes. It was a big job. We sprinkled the clothes wrapping them in a wet dishtowel, set up the ironing board and took turns ironing.

By the end of the day we were tired, but we thought nothing of it. The work ethic was so ingrained into us we just worked, not even thinking of shirking our duty. Sometimes we listened to the radio, but most of the time Anna didn't want it on.

The irons were heated on the cook stove. We clamped the handle onto the iron, pressing the clothes. When the iron cooled, we exchanged that iron for a hot one. Our clothes were made of cotton in those days and nearly everything we wore needed ironing, all except underpants and underskirts. By 4:30 and it was time for making supper the basket of moistened clothes was getting down to the bottom and we could rest, the scent of steaming clothes lingering in the air. The kitchen was warm, the humidity high. (Those antique irons make nice doorstops.)

After moving into town and merely throwing a switch or pulling a chain to throw light into the room we felt we had "arrived." We simply threw the switch and smiled! It was to be a new phase in our lives. I didn't take the "juice" in electricity for granted for a long time. When we moved into town and ironed clothes with the new irons we plugged into the wall I thought ironing was easy as sliding down a slippery slope.

Stephanie spoke up: "Tell me more, Gramma."

"Well," Anna smiled. "Washing woodwork was an important job for your mother and your Aunt Carrie when company was coming for Sunday dinner. I had painted the woodwork ivory and de kids had to scrub until it 'blitz-d-men-zoed'" (shone).

"We scrubbed it to a 'frazzle', nearly washing the paint off." I said, laughing.

Another task that has long since passed into history was washing the milk-separator. It was housed out in the milk house, along with the wash machine. I helped Barbie wash the separator a few times before we left the big farm.

Cleaning the cement floor in the milk house was a kick. Barbie and I scrubbed it with brooms, using hot water and detergent. We made it a fun job, chasing each other with the brooms!

The old-fashioned toaster was an interesting contraption. It consisted of four parallel wires about eight inches long, another wire running the perimeter of the appliance, with wire handles fitting together. We put the bread in, laid it on the wood stove, and (*voila!*) when the first side was toasted we turned it over. It was a marvelous invention! Seems crude today, but it did the job.

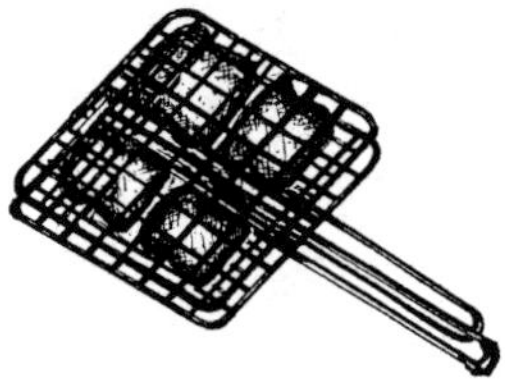

Anna had attended school only through the third grade and had not had a lot of courses in English. When we were talking in a group after dinner she might say: “I didn't finish my sentence.” Her sentences were quite long. She did love to talk. I think when she got to the pearly gates she may have told St. Peter: “I can't come yet. I didn't finish my sentence.” She was so neat in that respect. Another thing about her speech was how she rolled her 'R's. As I look back on it, *that* was hilarious.

We sat around and visited after meals often. I can see Rosie tipping his chair back on two legs while we chatted. On Sunday afternoons when Anna entertained I can picture the Rosenburg clan (including Helen, Sally and Albert’s families) sitting around the table talking state, national and world issues. It was a warm fuzzy feeling.

My mother had a mind for dates. During our high school years Carrie and I might be applying lipstick at the mirror in the dining room before going out the door. I can hear my Mom say: "Dis is my Mama's birthday," or: "Dis is my Papa's birthday." Grandparents on both sides were long gone before Carrie and I were even a glint in Edgar's eye. This small tribe was so busy with day-to-day tasks that forefathers were soon forgotten, but Mom always mentioned their birthdays. That's all we knew, that they had lived and died. I had never even seen pictures of them.

Dear Reader/friend: *I must tell you something* about Anna's mother, Dagmar, who would have been my Grandmother, had she lived longer. She must have been *very different.* Anna told me this story herself after I became a mother so it wasn't hearsay. She said Dagmar had had a baby lying in a crib. Someone told the mother there were tiny worms in the crib next to the baby! *(unimaginable!)*. When told about this situation Dagmar snipped, and I quote: "Oh, never mind, dere's more where dat one came from!" I could not believe it! I had always wished I'd had the pleasure to know my Grandmother. Now I wasn't so sure.

And I don't want anyone telling me this woman was of a different culture! Of course she was. But how anyone could have such wanton disregard for human life is quite beyond me. I know this wasn't indicative of the German people. This was a quirk of this individual whom I might have called "granny." How weird could she have been?

My mother had trouble pronouncing certain words. She was never able to say "February." It was always "Febuaar." Am sure this was due to her German heritage. Her birthday was

"Februaar" 5th. And speaking of that month, how she loved to tell us about Groundhog's Day! She never missed announcing the visit of the lowly groundhog. Legend had it that the groundhog came out of his hole on February second. If he saw his shadow we were in for six more weeks of cold weather. But if he couldn't find his shadow the weather would be more moderate. (Funny, I never noticed any difference as I grew up. We had freezing weather for another six weeks either way!)

Another word my mom had trouble with was 'yeast'. She was not able to sound the "y" and it was always "east." On bread-baking day she was very protective of her "east." This was part of her nature, and we wouldn't have had it any other way.

Following are a few of the common German phrases my mother used:

Ach du lieber grits: "Oh, for goodness sakes!"

- Huls' mul: "Keep your mouth shut."
- Sees' ta beta cooks: "Who's the best cook?"
- Ach him' mel: "Oh, heavens!"
- Sham' de vut: "Shame on you!"
- It's sum cra'zy varten: "Are you crazy?"
- Blitz da men zoes: "Shines"
- Fres: "Eat"
- Mench: "Good person"
- Schmect goot': "Tastes good!"
- Mein freert: "I'm cold. I'm freezing!"
- Grushion: "Money"
- Saleratus: "Baking soda"
- Dankeschoen: "Thanks a lot."
- Auf Wiedersehen: "Till we meet again."

Now I wish I had learned the language. Someone said to me recently: "The people who know only one language are called Americans." That holds an element of truth.

When mom was cooking she had a favorite saying: “There never was a pot so crooked that you couldn’t find a lid to fit!” I loved that.

Another facet of my mom, Reader/friend: She had a “thing” about washing her feet. No matter where she went she washed her feet first. If she and Dad went to visit the neighbors in the evening she put on a clean housedress and combed her hair. Then she got a basin, sat down and washed her feet. She'd put on clean stockings, hooking them to her garter belt. Then her shoes, and she was ready. It was a regular ritual with her. I don't know whether this was a carry-over from Germany or not.

Anna had many hobbies, but her first and ongoing hobby was *plants.* One would have thought she was in the plant nursery business, she had so many, both inside and outside. She dearly loved her houseplants and had the “greenest thumb” I had ever seen. Plants could be found all over the house, upstairs and downstairs. They stood on windowsills, benches, small tables, dressers; anywhere there was a flat surface and light.

Once I counted them. She had no less than one hundred, twenty-seven potted plants inside the house! This was when I was in high school. At that time the family had melted down to Carrie, Mickey and myself so my Mom had more time to devote to her plants. They do give off oxygen, so are nice in that way.

This love of plants has come full-circle. I love houseplants myself, mainly the large split-leaf philodendrons, cactus, and snake plants. But I can't make things grow like my mother could. She knew exactly what to do with her plants although she couldn't have told you what she did.

When in high school I felt that as far as plants and progeny went, plants took first priority with Anna. The way I saw it, she thought of her plants as wonderful children who stayed where she put them and never sassed back! And when conditions were right the more intelligent ones even bloomed! I can talk about it and laugh now but I couldn't in my salad days.

"Grandma, can you tell us something about yourself?" Stephanie queried.

"Well, sure. Somewhere along de line I lost my sense of smell. I can't smell a t'ing except de sweet scent of some flowers. I lost dat in my fifties, I guess. Dis never bothered me however. My other senses such as hearing and sight are still keen."

It came as a surprise to me to learn that my mother had had her ears pierced at one time. I'd never pictured her vain enough to have two more holes put in her head! But with so many mouths to feed, and another baby seemingly always on the way, who had time for earrings! And the little holes in her ear lobes had long since grown together. Dagmar may have had Anna's ears pierced when she was a child, who knows?

"What are some of your other hobbies, Grandma?"

"Well, jah, another t'ing I like is clocks. I like to hear de ticking of de clocks. After Dad passed away dey 'talked' to me." She collected clocks for years. She didn't listen to the radio, but loved to hear the ticking of the clocks. I must say it is not an unpleasant sound.

In my parents "later years" Esther, Francis and Roland had gotten dad and mom a television, something they had never had. But my mom never had time for TV. She liked to listen to two things in her home: the singing of the birds outside in the many trees and the ticking clocks on the inside! After dad passed she had the house to herself, and she created her own unique living arrangement. It was a kick!

My mom also loved mirrors. Wherever there was enough space on the wall my mom hung a mirror. She had round mirrors, square mirrors, rectangular mirrors and hexagon mirrors. She loved her mirrors. I think that's why she lived so long; she had so many interests. My mom lived to the venerable old age of 96.

When she visited us in Oregon she wanted to give me a gift of a mirror. I was not into mirrors, and told her I'd rather have a set of TV trays, so that is what we settled on. She felt bad that I didn't want a mirror, but for once in my life I had my own way.

Holidays were an important thing in the family. When I was small my Mom colored dozens of eggs for the Easter celebration. The night before Easter she filled everyone's cap (including the hired hand) with colored eggs and jelly-beans. She then hid the caps in the kitchen or dining room, not readily seen. One's cap might be by a cupboard door that was slightly ajar or around the corner of the woodbox. This must have been a custom from the Old Country. It was a fun thing, and we had hard-boiled eggs and toast for breakfast before getting ready for Sunday School.

And how she loved to paint! (walls). She'd get a big brush in her hands and paint everything in her path -- walls, woodwork and wainscoting. -- From the time I was nine it seemed Anna had a paintbrush in her hand at all times. She painted ceilings too. On the day she painted a ceiling she drank very little coffee. She didn't want to take time to get down off her bench to "go". And she used only brushes. She liked the "feel" of the brush and had never had a roller in her hands.

The bedrooms she painted a soft color of blue: aqua, pale blue or robin-egg blue. They were pretty. When "the girls" came home on vacation it was a standing joke whether mom would be wielding a paintbrush as she met them at the door! Fun! There is something to be said for large families. They had more fun!

I recall a story about Anna's painting: When I, Rootkin was eight, one Saturday night at eleven o'clock Mom came upstairs and roused me from sleep. She wanted me to come downstairs while she finished painting behind a large cabinet in the kitchen, needing to get it done so Dad could move the cabinet back in the morning. (She was scared. Somebody had driven into the yard, doused the lights and was sitting out there! -- We never locked doors and I doubt that the doors even had locks.)

So the sleepy-eyed Rootkin stretched, rubbed her eyes, and went down and "sat". After twenty minutes who should walk in but the ever-popular Esther! Her date had brought her home and they had been sitting out there necking! Some burglar, she!

My Mom loved to entertain! I felt she should have gone into business as a party-planner, that she had missed her calling. And when a crowd was expected for a special occasion she made her "egg coffee." It was delicious! I asked her how she made it.

"Well, it wasn't so different from regular coffee. I mixed de dry grounds with an egg. Den I put it on de stove in de big old enamel percolator." The gray enamel pot was 12 or 14 inches tall. It really was good coffee and she did this when she had a family dinner or a party.

Anna made her egg coffee when she entertained the Quilting Bee. In winter the neighbors got together at the different farm homes to tie quilts, passing the quilting frame around from one house to the next. The neighbors came in the evening with all kinds of desserts, and the children too. We kids played games and tried to keep out from under foot. It was a gay event.

The ladies gathered around the quilting frame on the dining table while their husbands talked politics in the parlor. We kids liked the banter of harmless chatter of the adults. It conveyed a certain ambience to the gala affair.

Sometimes we kids squeezed through the sea of legs and sat under the dining table. We couldn't understand what the mothers were saying, with so many different voices speaking at once, but it was a fun evening. – (We kids smiled and gave each other knowing glances under the dining-room table.) -- Rather than fleeing South for the winter these people tied quilts.

I recall the time a salesman named Mr. Mann came to our house selling Wearever pots and pans. He claimed these miraculous aluminum pots could cook an entire meal for ten using just one hot spot on Anna's wood cook stove. Gas ranges were coming into vogue. This method of cooking, he claimed, would be the most economical on the new gas stoves.

He put a Dutch oven on the stove. Then a flat piece of aluminum with holes in it fit into the rim of that. On the flat piece he placed two "half-moon" pans with another Dutch oven inverted over the whole schmeer.

This guy didn't need to high-pressure Anna into throwing a party for the neighbors. She, being the gregarious type, gladly took him up on it inviting the whole neighborhood. She supplied the veggies and meat: onions, carrots, spuds and beef, while this guy played chef using his "can't-get-along-without-it' cookware. (What a deal!)

Everyone Anna invited showed up, and the evening was a smashing success. Anna received a percentage off when she bought the set. Others bought the pans as well and a pleasant evening was enjoyed by all.

My mom spent the entire evening calling the salesman "Mr. Mann." I hadn't an inkling that that was his real name. I thought she called him that because she was odd, and that he was a man. Ah well, such is the life of a child. Everyone agreed that Anna was the perfect hostess. Her dinner party had been an overwhelming success.

Whenever one of the Rosenburg kids was confirmed in the church, the minister and his family were invited to our house for Sunday dinner. I have fond memories of the time Carrie was a small child and just talking well. Somebody picked her up just as the preacher and his wife stepped inside the door. Little Carrie piped up with: "Gimme a beer!" *That* was a kick!

After moving into Sleepy Eye we lived just kitty-corner across from the church so the minister, his wife and four small girls didn't have far to come. That was Pastor Eschenbachor, the same minister who confirmed me; he confirmed most of Anna's children. He was the kind of cleric who would sit down and enjoy a glass of wine in company, and was truly loved.

The pastor's wife always knew the correct thing to say. Once it was summertime and all the doors and windows were open wide. Our neighbor across the street was hammering something. He must have hit his thumb when suddenly he let go with a string of expletives. The words seared the air. We had sat down to eat, and had just said grace when his curses rent the air. The preacher's wife said in a calm cultured manner: "His voice certainly carries!" We laughed, and that saved the day.

After the last of the lemon pie crumbs were polished off, my Dad went into the parlor and lit a cigar. I have satisfying memories of this. Lots of people don't like cigar smoke, but for me it conjures up good feelings, pleasant chatter and all the ramifications of good times enjoyed mentally and spiritually.

The church I was confirmed in has since been razed and a new much larger one built in its place. Posted in the entryway are the names of the charter members of the church. When I was there attending my mother's funeral I saw my dad's name: "E.M. Rosenburg" along with five or six other charter members. The new church has stained-glass windows and lovely laminated beams, a tribute to God. Also, the new church echoes chimes every evening at six o'clock, something my mother appreciated.

She had always liked the location of her home because it is so close to St. Paul's Lutheran church. Also, there was a little corner store directly across the street where a widow-lady sold eggs, milk and baking items. If Anna needed something for her baking she could boogie over and pick it up. – The location was also nice for us kids because the Sleepy Eye High School was only a short two blocks away.

I must tell you, Reader/friend, about my mother's potato pancakes. She absolutely loved to make these, whipping up a batch at the tap of a pan! A German dish, we as good Germans, relished them. She grated her potatoes by hand. Even after blenders became popular she still preferred grating the potatoes by hand, frying 'em with just enough grease in the pan to make the edges crinkly. She served polish sausage and applesauce with her tater pancakes. They were the best!

And nobody had a weight problem. When God was passing out plumpness we girls were outdoors walking on stilts. -- Consequently we remained, like Anna, skinny as skeletons. (Well, not quite.) This prompted my brother-in-law to remark facetiously: "Sleeping with one of the Rosenburg girls is like sleeping with a picket fence!"

When my mom had a lazy day with nothing much planned she made doughnuts. She liked the raised doughnuts best; no cake doughnuts for her. They were placed on flat surfaces to raise: atop the warming ovens of the range, and on the table. We even set up the ironing board putting towels on that. -- She fried the fat spongy pastries in deep fat in a black iron skillet. Carrie and I dipped the doughnuts in granulated sugar. They tasted extra good just out of the hot liquid grease, and how we loved the doughnut-holes! Ummm, good! My mouth waters just thinking about 'em!

Now I'm getting a mental image long ago forgotten. Big people are fighting with angry words. Rootkin is standing off to the side by the woodbox next to the kitchen door as she is the silent witness to this -- not very old -- perhaps three or four. (I was so quiet I blended into the woodwork. Nobody noticed me.) Anna is foreman of this crew as they are cutting up beef after butchering. The beef carcass lays on the table ready to be cut up and salted down for good winter eating.

Across the table from the mother stand two of my big sisters, Frankie and Esther, wielding razor-sharp butcher knives. A noisy quarrel ensues between Anna and "the girls." There is commotion and angry talk; it is not a happy scene. -- The sisters are telling Anna where to go!

Anna puts out her fingers as if talking with her hands. Suddenly her middle finger, left hand, is slashed! Red blood spurts in all directions! Up the walls and down the floor! Which knife had sliced into her finger no one knew there was so much commotion. "Now look what you made me do!" she wailed, moaning in a high-pitched tone. Her daughters looked wide-eyed, momentarily not knowing what to do. My Mother moaned and moaned, not one to suffer pain silently.

After Frankie and Esther got over the initial shock of seeing blood spattered over the kitchen they had presence of mind to wrap a white "turkey towel" (Turkish towel) around Anna's blood-squirting finger. The Sleepy Eye doctor was called. He arrived post-haste with his little black bag. Dr. Will advised Anna she must be careful not to put her hand in cold water. A nerve had been severed, and if she used cold water the finger would go stiff. Well, Reader, my mom couldn't keep her hands out of cold water and the finger, as predicted, went stiff.

She was never able to bend her middle finger, left hand, from that day forward. -- Who would rinse the clothes before putting them into the washer, if not she! Not one to shirk her duty my Mom did what she had always done, pre-scrubbing the stained clothes and rinsing them in cold water. I was so young I never remembered her any other way but I was pretty observant, watching the entire scene. It is indelibly etched in my memory. I doubt whether the players in this little drama know to this day that I was there watching the scene play out.

When asked to sit for a photograph there was no problem. Anna simply placed her right hand over her left. That way no one knew the difference. And, true to her inner being, she was never one to let a stiff finger stand in her way of having fun!

When "the girls" - Frankie, Esther, and Barbie - were still at home I can hear Anna say: "You wash de dishes, you scrub de floor, and you wash de separator, while I do de 'real' work." What the "real work" was nobody knew. Unless it was baking bread and painting walls! If that's what it was, no wonder she called it the "real work."

ANNA'S GEESE

This story proved to be so fascinating that Stephanie flew out to the West Coast and worked at her job for a while. Then she quit working, flew back to Sleepy Eye, and continued her talking engagement with my mom.

"Tell me about the geese, Grandma. I've seen pictures of you and your geese. Can you tell me about that?"

"Jah, all right. Dat was such a fun time in my life. Well, I had worked in de house all my married life except for tending my flower garden, serving meals to everybody from t'reshing crews to visiting dignitaries from de church. At dis pa'ticular time I looked back with a sense of satisfaction at my family. I felt dat I had achieved a certain status in life.

One day I was outside digging in de dirt, planting bulbs for spring color. I pondered: 'I haven't earned any money dat I can call my own since I was a young lady. De good Lord knows I've done everyt'ing else.' I looked to de east, den turned my plaid-scarved head to de west, looking off to de horizon, saying to myself: 'I've been such a success at raising children. Even Mickey is well on his way to becoming a man. Maybe I should try somet'ing new!'

Mulling dis over for a couple weeks I finally told your grandfather I wanted to 'branch out'. Grampa must have been having a good day. 'What kind of business did you have in mind?' he asked in a courtly manner.

Well, I t'ought raising a few geese would be fun. Dey pretty much take care of demselves. When brand new dere nice to look at, and fun to touch, all fuzzy and warm. Dey have webbed feet so dey keep dere balance well. And we would never have to buy dem glasses. De only goose I've seen wear glasses was de original Mudder Goose. -- When 'Dad' agreed to dis business venture I went right ahead planning for de little goslings, doing everyt'ing myself. I bought the goslings in de spring, selling dem in de fall making a nice profit."

My Mom truly loved her geese. She would have even used the hiss if she could have found a use for it! Not only were the geese good to eat, but Anna used the "down" to make pillows. The feathers were used to make our feather beds. Also, she liked the wings to clean corners in the stairway.

When Carrie and I played "house" outside under the shade trees we learned to steer clear of the geese. If we were in the yard, anywhere near the gander he'd stretch out that old neck like it was elastic, hiss and point his yellow bill making the *frutzen* (brats) run.

Anna picks up her story: "One summer fourteen of de half-grown geese wandered off in de middle of summer. I pondered all dose weeks what had become of my "babies." Every time I counted dem I came up fourteen short. I wondered if dere was a fox out dere gaddering geese! Den along towards fall, when de leaves were turning color, imagine my su'prise when on de t'irteenth of August, Carl's birt'day, the now-grown geese came back, padding into de yard! Dey were healt'y and fat, 'talking' happily to their brothers and sisters. Dey had found grain in a distant field. Nearby was a pond where dey had gotten water. Dey were de picture of health."

On Thanksgiving Day it was customary for the Rosenburgs to feast on goose. I still like the taste of goose, maybe because I was raised on it, though I prefer the traditional turkey to the greasy goose.

The pictures of my mom with her geese are really nice. She stands in the background with her walking stick, wearing a man's dark jacket. In the foreground stands a flock of sixty to seventy-five geese. She raised geese for about ten years.

One of the main efforts in the summertime was canning the bounty. I loved the summer for that. My mother was a chronic canner. Her kitchen was a cannery, fruits and veggies coming in the back door, peeled, sliced and diced, going out the porch door down to the cellar.

Barbie, Carrie and I helped Anna put up peaches, pears, plums, and apricots. Anna preserved every fruit she could get her hands on, including strawberries and raspberries. When putting up the fruit with syrup all day the linoleum would squeak with the sound: "stick-a, stick-a, stick-a" as we walked across it. Then it was time to do some tall housecleaning.

Succulent tomatoes she canned by the truckload, it seemed. -- After the family dwindled down to Barbie, Carrie, Mickey, and myself, my Mom didn't need to "put up" the five hundred quarts of fruit and veggies besides dozens of quarts of dills, and bread-and-butter pickles.

One morning it was 97 degrees in the shade. I was Anna's helper, preserving peaches. Barbie was "working out." The fun-loving Carrie was outside playing. Dad had brought home three crates of peaches from "The Golden Rule," the grocery store he frequented. The house held the fragrance of a peach orchard as the peaches turned a luscious color of pink and gold.

As I lazily peeled the slippery peaches I noticed the names on the blue Mason jars: Kerr, Ball and Atlas. I fantasized about a strong man named Atlas, daydreaming about some strong sons and perhaps a few strong women (not too muscular). Or maybe meeting a man named Ball, and playing a lot of tennis. Had heard of a movie star by the name of (Deborah) Kerr in a far-off place called Hollywood, but Hollywood could have been on some distant planet for all I knew.

I couldn't believe how nice and quiet it was that day, and I enjoyed slipping the skins off the golden fruit. It was so pleasant, not a sound to be heard except steam escaping the various and sundry kettles Anna pushed around on the blazing stove; finding the hottest spot for her canner. The kitchen was hotter than the Tropics as we mopped the sweat off our brows. -- With the peach peeled it went into a bowl of salted water, to ensure the fruit retained their color. Sometimes half a peach found its way into my mouth. It was a bit salty, so good. This was definitely a fun job.

Shelling peas was the most time-consuming job when canning. In early morning during the cool of the day, we picked the peas, then sat down on benches to shell them in the afternoon. Can "hear" the peas plinking into the pail while shelling, a tedious job. We shelled a lot of peas to get a quart full!

Fond memories come to me when I think about Anna 'putting up' dill pickles. She used the tall blue 2-quart jars. A head of dill on the bottom, then the scrubbed cucumbers, more dill about halfway, more cukes, and the salt, making sure it was not iodized. A garlic clove and pickling spices, the brine, and that was it. Carrie and I put on the rubber rings and the zinc lids.

Finally Anna tightened the caps with a wrench. Just another task accomplished by this multi-faceted woman, my mother.

Cabbage was the last vegetable in the fall to be harvested. The other fruits and veggies were done, giving Anna time to concentrate on her sauerkraut. In a corner of the kitchen stood a large crock with a plate on top. Anna placed a large rock on the plate weighing down the cabbage. By some miracle of nature mouth-watering sauerkraut was the end result of the fermenting and foaming cabbage.

As a kid I didn't like sauerkraut, but today it's one of my favorite foods. Anna took a head of cabbage and ran it back and forth across the blades of the kraut-cutter in record time. (She shredded cabbage like "they" shred papers in certain circles today.) A pungent scent emanated from the fermenting cabbage as the day drew nearer when it would be put into jars. -- When my mom shredded cabbage we kids ate the core. It was good...

Thinking of the kraut-cutter, Reader/friend, I must tell you how Anna disliked the antique dealers. They came around wanting to "buy" just about anything they could lay their eyes on. When they saw the old washboard and copper boiler they talked real sweet, trying to impress Anna with "folding money."

She pretended to act real pleased in the hopes they would get the heck out of there. Her acting was so real that if she'd been playing for an audience she would have surely gotten an award.

Thank the Lord she didn't let them into the dining room where sat her buffet with the gorgeous hand-painted bowls and platters, not a hint of a scratch on them. After Dad died, these precious dishes began disappearing. Every time one of "the girls" came home, china dishes disappeared. It was downright spooky.

In those days ladies made their own laundry soap. Anna had been saving tallow for months in preparation for making her soap. She mixed in a can of the deadly Lewis Lye. Then two of the men hoisted the heavy old iron soap kettle on top of the wood range and she cooked it. (I don't know the recipe, only that she used lye.) After cooking and cooling she cut the harsh soap into bars. These bars she pre-scrubbed clothes with before they went into the machine.

Making soap was an interesting process to watch. There was a jelly-like substance left in the bottom of the soap-kettle; this was discarded. - Talk about hard work! That it was! She made her own soap for years, saving every scrap of beef tallow.

Nary a thing was thrown away. The dogs got the table scraps and the pigs got the potato peelings. The only thing we couldn't use were rusty screws and bent nails. Most everything else could be sanded down and used again.

As for clothes, Carrie and I didn't have a lot of hand-me-downs. Clothes wore out before they got down to us since we were way down the line, numbers 9 and 10 of Anna's babies. Mickey was #11, or when counting the entire tribe he was #17.

I remember crying a lot when very small, but I look back on that time with a certain degree of fondness. Guess that's nature's way of making something good come out of childhood memories. My psychiatrist says a tendency to depression could have taken place to the very time I was born, especially since my mom also had problems with her nerves. At this writing my depression has lifted and I feel good, even very good most of the time. I haven't outlived my bipolar illness, but with the right medication I can live a decent and productive life.

When the temperature soared into the nineties and we kids would have melted had we slept upstairs Anna made a nice bed for us downstairs on the floor in front of the screen door. She put an old worn quilt on the linoleum with a sheet for us to sleep on. Those were merry nights indeed, the evening breeze cooling our bodies.

In summer dad fashioned an outside shower for my brothers and the hired men. He rigged up a metal barrel on a platform seven feet off the ground close to the windmill, filling the barrel with water. The sun heated the water and it was piped down to a wooden shower stall. The men could lather up and rinse off, a dandy way to go after working in the fields all day. They worked till sundown getting the hay in, planting or harvesting.

When the men came in from the fields for meals they'd go to the washstand, roll up their blue cotton shirt-sleeves and wash in the basin up past their elbows, swishing off the dust. They wiped on a roller-towel.

On the 4th of July my Uncle August, Dad's only brother, a lot older than Dad, paid us a visit. He rumbled into the yard in a black flivver. He wore a battered brown felt hat. In his mouth he clenched a stogie. In his hands he carried a cellophane bag of candy. --Uncle came bearing orange slices, old-fashioned black licorice, or rock-hard lemon drops, never making an appearance without candy. He shook hands all around, even to the smallest of us kids. We would have loved him whether he came bearing candy or not, but with the candy we had more fun.

His wife had died long ago and he'd been a widower for years. He was rather rotund; that's what made him so jolly. Actually, he seemed more like a grandfather than an uncle. Dad was never happier than when Uncle August came to visit. We kids hung back. Uncle was old, and he was big. We had to show a certain amount of deference to this man. In one way Uncle August was not a bit like my dad. -- He had sired only two off-spring, one girl and one boy. -- I have always felt a special kinship to him because my middle name is August. – Guess I was named after him.

Dad had gone into Sleepy Eye early that morning to get a keg of beer. I guess he thought a small keg once a year was a good thing for us kids. We could have all the beer we wanted. It was mostly foam, and that made it all the more fun! We blew the foam off the beer on to our brothers and sisters. It was a kick! Dad and Uncle August laughed about old times while we kids sprinted around the yard spouting beer! And getting a tad tipsy!

On Independence Day Dad always picked up three or four small flags putting these on the car. He was a very patriotic man with a deep love for his country. This was the early forties of the twentieth century and everyone was patriotic then. People in that rural area were glad to work and have enough to eat. In retrospect it was almost an ethereal time, when awakening in the morning was a blessed event, the day was something to be challenged and won.

The air was pure. People were honest. Our food was organic and nearly everybody was lean. The streets in Sleepy Eye were rolled up like sleeping bags at night. There was no television so people got off their duffs and got physical. We lived very simply. It was a sweet innocent life.

July was sweltering in Minnesota. – If Uncle August didn't come over for the holiday Anna packed a lunch, Dad bought bottled beer and we headed for Lake Miltona near Parkers Prairie. Mom would drink one glass of beer at the lake. Dad drank beer and we kids drank nectar. (Parkers Prairie was the birthplace of the legendary Fred Zinter and was the town where my mother grew up. I may have heard the Zinter name in passing when I was a girl but had no knowledge of the man who held such fervor for our mom that his passion could have warmed the lake!)

We kids could hardly wait to get there and were on pins and needles the entire way. That was lake country -- near Alexandria – an area of rolling hills and big lakes. While driving we went a little ways, saw a lake, sometimes on both sides of the road at once. The road would bend, and just around the bend was yet another lake! Then we knew why people called Minnesota the "Land O' Lakes."

At Lake Miltona we hung towels over the car windows, took our clothes off and "swam" in our panties, such harmless fun! Sometimes we even peed in the lake. That lake was so big it didn't even care!

When our lithe bodies had cooled, and the skin on our fingers was wrinkled, we had our lunch. Dad had removed the back seat of the car and used that for seating. Mom had brought along a tablecloth. She put that on the ground with the food in the center. We kids sat on the fringes of the tablecloth and enjoyed a fried-chicken picnic.

Some of the other kids had swimsuits, but most swam in their panties so we didn't feel "different." We were careful not to go too far out into the lake because we had heard there was a "drop-off" in Lake Miltona and we weren't taking any chances. Every year that lake claimed a few people -- children *and* adults.

We didn't learn to swim as kids; we just played in the lake. My older sisters took swimming lessons at the YMCA in the city and learned to swim as adults. I can swim a little, but have never been a strong swimmer.

My favorite lake in Minnesota is Mantrap, up north closer to the Canadian border. My father-in-law loved to go fishing there. Lake Mantrap is huge, with thousands of irregular inlets and coves. It can trap a man as swiftly as any wily female.

Once or twice in summer a band of twelve or fifteen gypsies came traipsing into the yard. They were mostly ladies, all very slender, probably from so much walking. The boys and girls were barefoot. The ladies wore peasant-style long dresses in pastel colors of pink, yellow and aqua. They wore two or three strands of beads, and their long black hair was combed and coiffed attractively. They were clean and neat.

They said a few words to Anna. She went straight to the cellar coming back with three or four jars of canned goods while they waited in the yard. We kids hung back and watched. They politely thanked her and went on their way. Where they slept nobody knew; I guess they could be called nomads.

The only peddler who found his way out to the Ranch was the Watkins man. An older man, he was very thin and walked with a definite limp. Emerging from his car he carried what appeared to be a small suitcase. Anna was always home to look at his wares. This man wore a dilapidated felt hat. He knocked and entered Anna's cluttered kitchen.

Upon opening the valise the aromas escaped like genies coming out of a bottle. Exotic scents tantalized our senses, fancy names of spices like cumin, curry powder, and cayenne pepper, real vanilla, lemon and maple extract. Anna bought vanilla as she did lots of baking, making everything from sour cream cake to lebkuchen, a German honey cake made with fruit and nuts. I think she felt sorry for this man, driving from one farm to another, maybe selling only one item, although the farms were not far apart and gas was cheap. He had a hard time of it, but then everyone had a hard time of it. The Depression was not too far behind; that was the norm.

On those scorching days of summer the cellar was the place to go. Down there it was dark and cool and we carried a flashlight. Our eyes feasted on the bounty of summer arrayed on old wooden shelves and tables: classic colors of red tomatoes and golden pears, green beans and peas.

It was a delightful place, a little dugout under one corner of the house. Off in a corner lay burlap sacks containing potatoes, carrots and onions. We even raised our own popcorn, shelling it off the cob and storing that in the pantry.

When the grownups needed a pop bottle for something in the kitchen they might ask us kids to clean one. These could be found down on the cellar floor filled with cobwebs and dust. We put a little water and a few pebbles in the bottle swishing it around to clean it. I recall that with a pleasant feeling.

Besides cellar doors, we had rain barrels in back of the house. Anna used the "soft" water for washing her hair and watering her plants. Mosquitoes hatched in and around the rain barrel big-time. -- A small asparagus bed stood next to the rain barrel, but no one ever picked it. It went to seed every year. Guess it wasn't enough to bother with.

This was back in the days when cars had running boards. It was a quieter, safer, saner era. But in those days we didn't have satellites in space whirling around the planet; and it was decades before man had walked on the moon. In those "olden days" all we knew for sure was that there was a *"man in the moon."*

Every day we took the water pail out to the windmill. If the wind was blowing, the windmill pumped our water. Otherwise we pumped it by hand. We had a white, enamel, long-handled dipper to drink from. It matched the white pail, with a narrow red line going around the top. Everybody used the dipper, kids, hired-men, and everyone; and we had no more than the usual number of colds and sore throats. It was a marvelous invention.

Drinking the cool, fresh well-water when we were parched was like the first drenching rain in the desert after a dry spell. Our cousins from Parkers Prairie always said we had good water. I didn't know what they were talking about. I thought water was water. Now I know what they meant. It tasted good.

With no electric power on the farm we had no fridge so what we did to keep our butter and cream cool was to put it in a jar with a tight-fitting lid. Dad had fashioned a wooden box contraption at the top of the well with a hinged lid for keeping the butter and cream in, an ingenious way to keep food items fresh and cool. In no way did it resemble the automatic ice-maker fridges of today, but it did the job. It's amazing what all can be done where there's a will.

In some small towns the people used "ice boxes." These had heavy, thick doors and walls and were kept cold with a large chunk of ice. -- Aunt Louise' husband, Uncle Harry, was the iceman over in Parkers Prairie. He kept the ice in a shed in a pile of sawdust, insulating the ice from the sun. He would hitch up one horse and a wagon, going from house to house selling ice. You might call it "the Good Ol' Days."

When we visited at Uncle Harry's and Aunt Louise' place they'd get out the Tinker Toys. Our cousins, Virginia and Lorraine put together fancy stuff with those, but they were something new to us. -- In later years Uncle Harry owned a big locomotive which he sold to the City of Parkers Prairie. It can be seen today in the village park.

In the summertime my mother wore the popular cap-sleeved dresses showing off her slender upper arms. She was so thin she looked almost frail, as if she would fall over if you shook your finger at her. But she was anything but frail. Physically she was a strong person, rising early in the morning, working hard, not resting until she went to bed at night. -- She had never worked outside with the animals as Dad's first wife had done, but she certainly "pulled her weight" inside.

When the "layered look" became fashionable we girls thought it was a kick. Anna had layered her clothes for years. She was truly a forerunner of fashion in the strictest sense. She'd put on a "middy", then a cardigan, a blouse, and then a vest and another sweater over that. "Who has more fun than people!" she'd say. Then she'd dance the little jig.

Her expressions were strictly her own, and she used some interesting words. One such word was "plinter." She might say to Carrie and me: "Be careful with your babysitting money, or before you know it you'll have it all *'plintered' away*." She knew what she was talking about there. -- During high school I did a lot of babysitting making thirty-five cents an hour. I'd always tried to save enough money to buy a sweater, but rarely was able to do it. Guess I had "plintered" it all away.

On an extra busy day Anna might say: "I am a busy body!" We loved it. I don't think she had heard that term meaning gossip. She meant she was a busy person. I had never seen her sit down to read until she was into her eighties. By that time she was reading the large print *Reader's Digest*.

If she looked for a pan or bowl in the cupboard, upon finding the article, she'd say: "I finally got my eyes on to it." An odd-shaped pan -- we had two shaped like half-moons -- she called "vessels." I can hear her say: "Give me that vessel." Nobody else called it a vessel, but we knew what she was talking about. And, we had been taught to respect our elders, even though we may not have approved of everything they did.

Often when she was baking a cake she would not be able to find the soda or baking powder. Then she'd say: "Can't I see?" When she started talking about it, she found it. Then she could be heard saying: "Oh, dere it is. I finally got my eyes on to it."

When we had the radio on for twenty minutes she might say: *"Turn off dat old 'blatt'-machine!"*

If I were looking in a drawer in the buffet where she kept her table linens she might say: "Oh, don't go 'mousing around' in dere!" Sifting through things in drawers was "mousing around."

Once I overheard her saying to someone: "Dat man was so friendly I t'ought he was a salesman." I loved it.

I was a very curious child. This next story takes place during World War II when sugar was rationed. The desk, (a "secretary") was a two-piece affair, the top half sitting on the lower half. It stood in the parlor.

The young girl Rootkin, pulled on the knobs of the lowest drawer about six inches off the floor. I pulled and pulled, but it was sticking and would not budge. I tugged on the drawer a little more, to no avail. Being a determined soul I strained, giving the drawer one more hard pull. With that, the drawer "gave" and fell to the floor with a thud, revealing the hidden treasure: two ten-pound sacks of rationed sugar!

As the drawer opened, weighted down with twenty pounds of sugar, the top section of the piece catapulted over my head and crashed to the floor, smashing the glass doors to bits!

I sat in the midst of it, the bottom half of the desk still standing before me, the top half to my rear, the glass in the doors shattered. Not moving a muscle I waited for the anticlimax to this little drama. I thought I'd "get it" for sure now, but don't remember any punishment.

Looking back on it I wonder why I hadn't gotten a lickin', but if it had been one of my own I would have considered it a case of being a little too curious. That must have been how my dad reasoned. -- He was the one who meted out the punishment. -- The sugar was perfectly good, still in its original sacks. *Was that ever a scare!* I remember it like it was last night.

And, Reader/friend: this was in the era of: "Children should be Seen and Not Heard." I actually *believed* that stupid rule, keeping my mouth closed, not speaking to anyone except my peers until I was grown! You better believe I never told my kids that. *"Seen and not heard" indeed!* How else will children learn to speak if never given a chance? I did not approve of that rule then and don't believe in it today. People who believe those idioms have never learned to think for themselves.

My Mother Anna and my daughter Stephanie

Author and younger sister Carrie.

Author, years of teaching second grade, Staples, MN.

My Mother Anna as a young lady before she married.

Aunt Louise - mother's sister.

"Mickey"-child #17-served in Vietman

Author in grade school photo.

All 12 sisters were present at my Mother's 90th birthday party. Front: sister Francis and mother Anna. Middle row, left to right: Barbara, Johanna, Selma, Sidonia, Martha, Hildie. Back row: Ruth, Clara, Carrie, brother Roland, Esther, Helen.

Chapter VI LIFE ON THE RANCH

My mother has now gone to her reward. Stephanie has long ago gone back to her employment in Seattle. I, Rudy, am telling "the rest of the story" for future generations.

Focusing on the old "home place" -- as Anna used to say -- visions of hollyhocks, red, yellow and blue fill me up. The tall slender flowers sway against the house, dancing in the wind. Clumps of pink and red peonies lend the air a heavenly scent, while fragrant purple lilac trees stand guard around the house. Adding to the ambience are three or four clusters of "smelling-leaves." These were spearmint, I now know, but Carrie and I called them "smelling-leaves." We picked a few on our travels around the yard.

Rocks formed the walls for our playhouses. Using wooden orange crates Rosie made us tables and cupboards. Santa had brought us china tea-sets for Christmas, the kind of china that shattered when it fell to the ground. These we placed carefully in the orange-crate cupboards. Orange crates also served as chairs for our "babies." Our playhouses were a fantasyland under the oak and spreading maple trees. In my mind I see Carrie and myself spooning peas into our dollies' tiny mouths.

We found an old broom that was worn down to the "quick" and swept the dirt floors of our playhouses. Gunnysacks lay on the floor for rugs. It was a magical time.

A few years later Dad made stilts for us. Those were fun as we pretended to be tall skinny people. We appreciated Dad making the stilts. Even after fathering so many children he still took time to make fun things for us.

On stormy days Carrie and I went up to the attic. We were in the primary grades in this setting. Through a small door perhaps thirty inches high, we went, ducking our heads to get in. Going to the smallish windows just below the apex of the roof we peered out at the world.

We liked to listen to the rain pelting the low-slung roof just above our heads. It sounded like hundreds of horses' hooves. Then I went to the small windows pressing my nose against 'em. We loved to watch the summer rainstorms. A streak of lightening lit up the heavens, and a split-second later we heard the clap of thunder! We were spellbound! The window may not have been the safest place to be but we had no fear at the time.

The attic was our own private hideaway. No one else ever came up there. On sunny days hordes of flies congregated in the windows. They liked the sun's warmth. The buzzing of the flies was a pleasant sound too, all part of the atmosphere of the attic.

From this vantage point we looked across the yard. On the far side stood the red barn. Close to the house on the left stood the white milk house and the windmill. The smokehouse was located behind the milk house.

Over to the far right was the long machine shed where Edgar had held romantic entrapments with his ladylove as she delicately found her way around the ranch. Two corncribs with fringes of grass around the buildings stood just beyond the machine shed. The center of the yard was bare of grass due to all the foot traffic, machinery clacking along, automobiles of the day and the horses being shod and hitched up. Activity of some kind was usually going on in the yard.

The most fascinating thing in the attic was an old navy-blue trunk. It was a veritable treasure-trove brimming over with fancy kid-stuff for us to pore over: doll-heads with eyes that opened and closed, beige-colored lace, hats with veils, navy-blue hats with long feathers, big sisters' cast-off dresses, coats with genuine fur, and spiked heels! Also naked doll bodies without heads, dolls my big sisters had loved and spanked. Oh, what precious junk could be found in the old trunk!

Carrie and I donned these fancy duds and sashayed across the road to Donna Denow's house. In high heels, long dresses and lacy shawls we promenaded. Those were the best of times. That farm was the happy place where the McQuillans had lived. The McQuillan girls were good pals of my sisters, Frankie and Esther, during the "roaring" twenties. The place was steeped in tradition.

At Donna's house we played between two lilac hedges about six feet apart. The lilac trees met overhead and it was shady and cool there. I recall "marrying" a neighbor boy by the name of Roy or Ray or something between the lilacs, a love-struck boy and girl promising to cherish each other forever. Donna Denow was the preacher man and Carrie was my maid of honor. My bouquet was dandelions and "smelling leaves."

After the ceremony we trekked over to the rusted automobile sitting in the tall grass, and "went to town." We cocked our hats in a provocative manner! Mickey drove, but if he wasn't around one of us girls dressed as a boy and she "drove." Women's Lib at its finest! We honked the horn and vicariously sped down the road. It was a splendiferous day!

One day when I was perhaps five or six I was at home in the pantry and discovered where the raisins were kept. Taking a handful outside I gobbled them up greedily. Sneaking back for more I went to the pantry again and again, grabbing a handful of raisins, then returning to the great outdoors to enjoy them. They tasted extra-good, maybe because I'd gotten them on the sly! Nobody said anything about it. Don't think it ever was noticed.

After my older siblings were gone from home "working out" I recall my dad playing with us three still at home. This was in the evening after supper. Carrie, Mickey and I climbed on Dad's knee. Then he straightened his leg, and his knee collapsed. We laughed till our sides ached. Then we climbed on his knee again. Once more he relaxed his leg and we guffawed. He loved to play with his babies and I think he did this with all of them.

After a few minutes Anna came in to the front room to say it was bedtime. We laughed harder. -- She scolded dad: "Now look what you've done! You've got those kids so wound up I can't do a t'ing with 'em!" Amid squeals of laughter we climbed on his knee one more time, laughing until tears came to our eyes. -- This situation after they had produced eleven children together. -- He and she complimented each other at times.

I recall an old brown leather couch that dad called "the lounge." Carrie, Mickey and I romped on that with my father when we were very small. The leather was badly worn off in places. Guess dad got rid of it because it's not in my memory during my grade school years.

Another thing we three did when we were just small "sprouts" (Carrie, Mickey and I) was to sleep together in a double bed. And you know, Reader, when we grew up we didn't have a bit of trouble deciding which sex we were! Little brother, Mickey, was very hot-blooded. Carrie and I called him "the stove." If we were cold we cuddled up to him. This was when I was perhaps four. Before long Mickey would bunk with Rosie.

I was scared to death of kidnappers. After hearing much on the subject -- the Lindbergh baby had been kidnapped at that very time -- I'd lie in bed at night wondering. If they, the kidnappers, came to our house, which kid would they take? Would they kidnap the girl in the middle, or the one on the "outside" of the bed. Or would they reach way over and take the kid sleeping against the wall? That was a big concern of mine.

Going back into the corners of my mind where we never forget, I'm reminded of a word game Carrie and I played in bed. The first player might say: "I went to the city and saw a bear." The next player had to think of an animal beginning with the last letter in bear. This being "R" the second player might say: "I went to the city and saw a rhinoceros." Then skunk, and so on. We called this game "cumjy-cum." It occupies a happy place in my mind.

Over in the far corner of the bedroom stood the white enamel "tepee" like a sentinel. Guess that's German for thunder-mug. The tepee had a thin catalog on top for a lid. Worked fine on long freezing nights when the temperature dipped into minus degrees Fahrenheit. The catalog served a dual purpose. It also was our toilet paper. The privy was outside and if we'd gone out there we would have frozen our buns off!

The climate seems to have changed as the winters are quite temperate now at the turn of the new century, but in the nineteen-thirties winters were akin to going to Antarctica for a few months. There's been a noticeable change of seasons in Minnesota, perhaps not every year but some years it has. I believe the temperatures are affected by global warming.

Minnesota is known as the Gopher State, but I remember when the "they" people were toying with the idea of calling the state "Theater of Seasons." Guess the new nickname never caught on. That would have been an apt description of the state, however. -- Minneapolis celebrated summer with the Aquatennial for as long as I can remember, and in winter while we kids built igloos out of ice and snow, Minneapolis celebrated the Ice Capades.

Autumns were glorious with the fall season stepping forth in her new apparel, while spring blossomed lovely and cool.

In winter we were glad to have the feather beds that Anna fashioned of goose feathers and down. It was the only thing we knew. The feather bed was our mattress and was much like the comforters of today.

Thinking about my mother making our feather beds reminds me of the time that she was making pillows to give as a wedding gift. She was patiently stuffing "down" into the ticking case. We were all sneezing, but she still had the patience for it. Finally Mickey said: "Oh, Ma, why don't you give them the feathers and let them make their own pillows!" Out of the mouths of babes…

Dad was handy with a hammer and nails. Besides benches for seating at the table he made two-tiered benches for my Mom's ubiquitous plants. I can picture the bay window in the front room, Dad's two-tiered bench holding the radio and Anna's plants. I recall the old wooden telephone hanging to the right of the window, sunshine flowing through.

One weekend Esther was home from the cities. She gathered Carrie, Mickey and myself around the radio, tuning it to a special program, Let's Pretend. With shining eyes we listened as this rich baritone voice came over the air telling fairy-tales geared to preschoolers.

The male voice brought us visions of castles, fairies, and above-the-real-world fantasies. Esther watched to see our reactions to the program. We sat mesmerized by fairy tales that transcended space to come into our home. Many were stories we'd heard before, but they took on a richness of feeling and imagination coming over the radio.

It was with great anticipation that Carrie and I looked forward to my big sisters coming home for the weekend. Since they were working in the Minneapolis/St. Paul area we didn't see nearly enough of them. Dad waited for the Greyhound bus at the DX station in Sleepy Eye. It was 9 o'clock in the evening when they returned to the ranch. We could hardly wait for them to drive into the yard. Exciting times we had when Clara, Francis and Esther came home for a holiday.

We loved to see their suitcases lying open: all these glamorous clothes spilling out, filmy scarves and leather belts, smelling of cologne, and a faint aroma of smoke. Once I had gotten into Frankie's lipstick. I remember turning it up, to see how it worked. Suddenly it broke off! I was scared to death! When she discovered the broken lipstick she questioned me about it. I kept repeating: "No, I hadn't done it!" I think that taught me not to mess around with other people's property!

There was the time that "the girls" had come home for the weekend. "Clarie" was combing my hair; it was crackling and standing on end. She said: "Look at all the electricity in Ruthie's hair! Look at the 'lectricity in Ruthie's hair"..... I stood there thinking it all quite wonderful as I turned round and round, looking like a dandelion gone to seed.

Like all the other farm families of that era Anna had gotten one of the stately Aladdin lamps when those came into vogue. The grand lamp was placed in the center of the table. It was elegant with the mantle and the tall chimney. All studying stopped when Anna lit the magic lamp. The flame burned through the mantle. The mantle flared up and made a hiss and a shushing sound all at once. Then it settled down and burned brightly. It illuminated the entire room, not just the immediate area. Funny, many years ago now, my mom had it converted to electricity to keep up with the times. Those are collectibles now.

Still reminiscing, I see Anna go to the wooden telephone. She turned the crank a couple times. When "Central" came on the line she said very distinctly that she wanted The Creamery, where Dad worked. A few seconds later we heard her say: "Is E.M. dere?" She left a message. A few minutes later Dad returned her call. The phone rang two "shorts" and a "long."

Anna picked up the phone and could hear everyone on down the line, the "rubbernecks," pick up their receivers. This was a "party line" with six or seven parties on the same line. "Click, click, click" went the line as the party-liners picked up their phones. Then our very own Anna ordered whatever she needed from town. By this time the rubbernecks had a good idea what Anna was planning for supper, but she was just independent enough that she didn't care.

No one had any privacy on the party-line but this was decades before the invention of TV. Listening on the phone added zest to the people's daily living. It was a real-life happening, and everyone wanted to get the latest installment on the live soap-opera. Uninvited people were privy to everything from light-hearted banter to sad dramatic situations. We didn't mind the rubbernecks listening in. But it was a clear insult when they hung up in the middle of a conversation as if to say it wasn't worth listening to!

Now, Reader/friend, I'd like to tell you about Sunday dinners at the Rosenburg Ranch. I'll begin with Rosie. -- When company was coming for Sunday dinner my brother went out to the chicken house the day before, coming back with four or five roosters in a gunny sack. (The hens were saved for laying eggs.)

I remember one Saturday in summer I'd had a bath in the round galvanized tub in the kitchen. -- We put towels over straight-back chairs and set those up for screens around the tub. I had gotten dressed and had had a shampoo in a basin. Here am I sitting on the stoop all bright and shiny, glistening in the sun, my skin clean and fresh, my thin hair dripping as it dried.

Rosie came out of the chicken yard carrying a gunnysack that was jerking this way and that, as it contained live chickens. Picking up the axe, he went over to an old tree-stump behind the milk house, laid the head of the rooster on the old stump and chopped off its head! What a sight! It was hilarious to see the silly chickens jumping around sans heads! A reflex action made them teeter on one foot, then the other, before dropping over. I couldn't help but giggle at the silly chickens. Then I knew what people meant when they said: "She looked like a chicken with its' head chopped off!"

A tub of boiling water Anna had at the ready. The big galvanized tub stood on a bench behind the smokehouse. Filling the tub with scalding water from three teakettles, we doused the roosters all over and quickly plucked off the feathers. Everybody helped with the plucking. We worked fast. With the chickens naked they were taken inside and singed over the open flames of the cook stove. Anna did the butchering.

Little sisters always look up to their big brothers and I certainly did. When I was out playing and an airplane came into view I recall Rosie saying: "Ruthie, look up there," pointing to the sky. "See the airplane!" It was just a tiny speck in the sky.

The Wright brothers had invented their flying machine in 1903 in Kitty Hawk, North Carolina and were making great strides in air travel by 1914. When I was born in 1931 planes in the air was a common sight. -- Orville and Wilbur Wright would cough and roll over in their graves if they saw the giant jets of today. Their first experiment in the air had their plane going about thirty miles per hour..........

Another thing Rosie did for the entertainment of us younger kids was to take a pail of water and swing it up over his head without a drop spilling out! That was fun to watch as it demonstrated the principle of centrifugal force.

The potato-dicing scene was a fun thing. Frankie, nine years my senior, and Rosie are the two players here. They sat on chairs with the backs cut off on the front porch on the little farm. We lived there only briefly, about a year and a half. Rosie and Frankie are dicing potatoes for spring planting.

Rosie had gone down to the cellar with this beat-up dented wire potato bucket bringing up the soft shriveled spuds with long sprouts from the previous year. The sprouts looked like tentacles of a shriveled octopus. He and Frankie are dicing the potatoes into small kegs. Frankie doesn't live here anymore. She works in the "twin cities," but is home for the weekend.

Across the top of the kegs were blades placed like the lines in a game of tic-tac-toe. They put a potato on the blades, then hit it with a wooden mallet to dice it. Each piece of potato had an "eye," or two or three. From the "eye" the new plant grew.

Frankie was guessing the make and year of the cars going by on the "washboard" gravel road, mostly Fords and Chevies in those days. After the dust cleared Frankie made a wild guess, her lusty laughter filling the air. She usually got the make correct but had trouble with the year. Rosie, the omniscient big brother always knew. He was quizzing her; I was playing nearby. Or maybe I was only observing, not wanting to miss anything.

I never talked much but did like to watch what was going on. I can see the dust the cars create as they drive along the road. The cars moved slowly, and there were fewer of them.

There's another good tale about Frankie. My folks had received many lovely wedding gifts. They were beautiful indeed, lovely hand-painted bowls and a fourteen-inch diameter hand-painted cake plate. Also a crystal footed cake plate for Anna's layer cakes. These are in mint condition to this day, never having been used. She did use the footed cake plate for layer cakes on birthdays, however.

My parents also received an exquisite cut-glass pitcher with matching tray. This was the authentic cut-glass. -- There were no cheap imitations in those days.

Frankie is the only player in this episode. Since this was in the days before "running water" Frankie was taking water from the reservoir to wash her hair, using the cut-glass pitcher. The basin was sitting on a high bench in preparation for her shampoo. Things were progressing nicely when she struck the lovely pitcher sharply against the reservoir smashing the pitcher to smithereens! It was not a pleasant thing to see that *genuine cut-glass piece* in a million pieces!

But we were not ones to cry over spilt milk, spilt coffee, or even spilt cream so we didn't cry over cut-glass pitchers either. We didn't cry over anything. Even I had out-grown the crying stage. That was the end of the pitcher, but we still had the matching tray. We were thankful for that. That's still in one piece with no nicks or scratches.

When my mom washed clothes she used lots of starch. She said clothes stayed clean longer that way. Our clothes were made of cotton and nearly everything needed ironing. -- The hankies invariably got mixed in with the basket of clothes to be starched and we had to blow on these stiff little squares of fabric. And she believed in using lots of "bluing." She rinsed the clothes twice, once with bluing in the water. Anna said that way the towels and sheets didn't "yellow." I still have the bluing bottle she gave me. It's a small bottle perhaps five inches high with the words: "Mrs. Stewart's Bluing" embossed into the glass.

Once Barbie and I were out in the milk house washing clothes. She is just older than I in the pecking order. The milk separator was housed there; also various cream cans, milk cans and milk pails. On the walls hung round galvanized washtubs in several different sizes.

Also housed in the milk house were the wash machine and wringer, powered by a Briggs and Stratton motor. And I mustn't forget Anna's old washboard and "wash-stick."

The wash-stick was an old broken-off broomstick so old and tattered it was full of splinters, five or six inches long. We were careful where we touched that. Actually, my Mom was the only one who used the wash-stick, dipping it down into the scalding water, pulling out soiled clothes. She laboriously used the scrub board on the soiled spots before they went into the regular wash.

Barbie and I put the clothes into the agitating wash machine, washing the white clothes first, then the coloreds, and lastly the dark clothes and blue jeans. We thought we were quite modern, having the motorized washer and wringer.

After agitating, the clothes went into a tub of cold water for rinsing. We sloshed them through the cold water; then put the clothes through the motorized wringer.

Once we had a real emergency! The clatter of the Briggs and Stratton motor was so earsplitting we had to shout above the din in order to be heard. Barbara stood at the washtub feeding clothes into the wringer. I was in the milk house keeping her company. All of a sudden Barbie's thick shoulder-length dark hair *got caught in the wringer pulling her head up to the rollers! She hollered, twisting her head every which way, to no avail. There was a release on the wringer somewhere, but we didn't know where it was. Alarmed, I ran to the house -- ten or fifteen feet away on the cement walk -- for help.*

Esther came out, hitting her hand sharply on top of the wringer, freeing Barbie. She had lost a clump of hair, but said she was okay. <u>That</u> was a scare! After that incident we were a lot more careful when using the wringer. It was like a woman-eating animal if we didn't watch what we were doing! When I said my prayers that night I thanked God for putting me out there where I was able to run for help.

I was notorious for stepping on rusty nails sticking out of boards in the summertime. I don't think a summer went by that I wasn't on crutches. Going barefoot was fun, and boards with nails sticking out lay all over down by the barn. My feet took on a magnetic quality when boards lay around, rusty nails poking through. The disinfectant bottle danced out of the closet. A drop or two in a basin of lukewarm water twice a day worked like magic and I never got lockjaw. - Don't know why I wasn't more careful. Guess I was carefree and didn't watch where I was going. About the only time I wore shoes in summer was on Sunday when attending church.

When I was seven I burned my foot badly. -- Anna had placed a pan of scalding water on the kitchen floor. Just then the phone rang and she went into the "front" room to answer it. I ran into the kitchen stepping into the scalding water with one foot.

Immediately I put my foot in cold water to quell the burning. My mom admonished me that I should not have done that; that I should have smeared lard or butter on the burn. Now we know we should put the coldest water available on a burn. (I give myself a mental pat on the back for having done the right thing.) Butter, with all that salt would have been painful.

The next story is a happy scene, Reader/friend. Rosie is out in the cowbarn milking. We had only about fifteen cows at this time and Rosie is the only person milking. The hired men are gone and my big sisters have gone to the twin-cities. As the family dwindled down, so did the herd. The cows had names like Mazie, Fanny, and Daisy, many rhyming at the end. This was the era before milking became mechanized. Rosie sits on a three-legged wooden stool while milking. I am there playing with the kittens. The cowbarn had a pleasing feeling.

It is the "deep" of winter. The barn is steaming because of all the cows in their stanchions. They are letting off loads of steam and they stomp from time to time. Rosie is pulling on the cow's titties, the warm milk squirting into the pail he holds tightly between his legs. His left knee is up against Mazie's back right knee. If the cow switches her tail Rosie twists it good and tight, holding it in place on bossie's leg with his left knee. The cow stands perfectly still, glad to be relieved of her full "bag" of milk.

In my mind I hear the milk as it squirts into the pail. It starts out with the raw milk making a high-pitched squirting sound as it hits the empty metal pail. As the pail fills, the squirting takes on a more muffled sound. Then as it gets closer to the rim it has a mellow sound. With the pail almost full, and heavy, Rosie sets it down on the cement floor. It doesn't take long for him to finish. Then he empties the pail into a milk can.

When Rosie goes on to the next cow, "Dottie," he says: "Ruthie, watch this!" With that he points the cow's tittie towards the cat dish, squirting it full with warm milk for the cats and kittens. They come a-running pell-mell, five or six skinny cats in different colors: calico, orange, black and white. The cats hung around the barn and hunted field mice. -- The dog had his own house up closer to the people-house. I recall a dog named Fido, a short-haired yippy dog. Later on we had a dog named Storm, a rottweiler. He was the dog I loved, very protective. Both were good when the cows needed rounding up.

Winter came early one particular year. It was late October and the wind bit your nose and ears. Scarves were a necessity unless we kids were inside the barn. The cowbarn was warm, but I complained to Rosie that my hands were cold. He beckoned for me to come over to him, putting my hand in between Mazie's leg and her warm "bag" of milk. Instant warmth for cold hands!

The milking scene was all very pleasant, the milking, the kittens lapping up the warm milk, and the scent of fresh hay pulled down from the hay-mow.

As the nights were long in winter, everything was done by the light of a lantern. Now I see Rosie carrying the lantern while pulling the milk cart from the barn to the milk house. He saunters across the yard making grotesque shadows as the lantern dances crazily in the darkness.

The milk was run through the separator. The cream, being lighter, rose to the top. Dad took the cream cans into town, to the creamery, the following day. There it was processed into butter.

We kids liked to go up to the haymow and play in the hay. But we knew there were holes we could fall through so were careful where we stepped. It was a fabulous place. We climbed the ladder to get up there. It was great fun exploring the haymow mysteries. Now I feel like I should have spent more time there, playing longer. Always felt not enough hours were spent playing in the hay-mow.

We moved into town when I was in sixth grade, just before the Rural Electric Association (REA) came into being, giving electricity to that rural area. -- The farms were much much smaller than today's farms. Actually, there's no comparison.

When I was just a little tot I had wandered down to the barn one morning. The men had just gotten the horses harnessed up to do field work. One of the mares had a foal following along with his mother. The hired-man picked me up and put me on the foal. Seconds later the baby-horse bucked and I went flying high in the air! Gordon – the hired man -- caught me in his arms on the way down! After all these years I remember it the scene.

Another time Carrie, Mickey and I decided to ride the small mare, Nellie, the mother to Tom. Dad used that team, Tom and Nellie, the most on the little farm. – We three were out in the pasture and we came upon Nellie. Thinking it might be fun to ride, we got the old mare over by a stump, climbed on the stump, then we all three clambered on Nellie's bare back.

She was a small horse, and she was old and tired. She took us along towards the barn, doing a slow gait. (We thought we were really smart, all on the mare at once.) When we came to this little creek -- a mud-hole, really -- she bucked us off! All three of us fell in the muddy creek! Nellie may have been old, but she was still smart! That time I should have gotten a lickin', but all I got was a good talking-to!

All children are cute, and Mickey was no exception. When he was four Dad brought home a small short-haired black and white dog. The next day Mickey was outside with a 9-foot bamboo stick poking at the puppy while the dog hid behind a big barrel. When we asked him what he was doing he replied: "Dad said that's a watch dog. I don't want him watching around me!"

Then there was the time Mickey was told to sit up to the table; we were ready to eat. At that moment he hollered: "Gordon Larke wants me!" putting special emphasis on each syllable in the hired man's name, scooting into the front room to Gordon as fast as his little legs could carry him. So cute!

My mother's younger sister, Emma, had married a photographer. When I was seven Anna took a trip down to see Aunt Emma in Albert Lea. Mom wanted me to go with her, begging me to go, but I was having "none of it." I had always been a very sensitive child and didn't trust people, even some members of my own family. So Anna had no choice but to take Carrie.

They put on their happy togs, my mom wearing her lovely emerald ring with the three small stones. Anna and her "baby girl," as she called Carrie, boarded the Greyhound bus in Sleepy Eye. They planned to change buses in the cities. They had a good time on the bus, and upon arriving in the Minneapolis depot Anna and Carrie went to the "biffy." When they returned to the terminal a woman went running through the crowded depot like a bear was chasing her! Carrie said to Mom: "Ma, look at her run! Ma, look at her run!"

The upshot of the story was that my mom, who had never traveled by herself, had forgotten her purse in the toilet stall. And the running-woman had found it! – *She thought she had hit the jack-pot!* The purse contained forty-seven dollars, which was bad enough; but even worse, Anna and Carrie's return tickets were in the purse!

Anna was understandably upset. A kind lady with a soothing voice came up to talk to her. My Mother had presence of mind to tell her that Sidonia, her daughter, lived in nearby Rochester. This lady telephoned Sid who drove to Minneapolis that very afternoon to pick up Anna and Carrie, driving them down to Albert Lea. So my Mom didn't miss a single day of her visit.

Several days later the purse miraculously appeared. The thoughtful thief had dumped it in a mailbox. Authorities found Sid's address inside and had mailed the purse to her. The bus ticket was still intact; everything was there except the money. Forty-seven dollars does not seem like much today, but was a tidy sum in Anna's world. I think one of God's angels must have been watching over her to have everything turn out so well.

When the men were still at home I remember dad calling them in the morning. They didn't use alarm clocks. Perhaps my dad did, I don't know. But at the crack of daybreak dad stood at the foot of the stairway calling: "Fred, roll out! Carl, roll out! Gordon, roll out! Roland, rollout!" He waited five minutes. If the men didn't stir, dad started over calling them again. On the second call he usually got better results.

In my reverie I'm getting a mental image of the hired-man, Gordon. He stands just around the corner of the barn "cupping" his hands, rolling a cigarette out of the wind. The tobacco falls into the tiny thin paper. He shifted it "just so," then moistened it with his tongue to seal the cigarette. Finally he pulled the little string with his teeth to close the tobacco pouch.

Ranch hands and cowboys rolled their own cigarettes in those days. Another thing I liked to watch was my brothers and the hired men lacing up their boots. They wore high boots that came to the knee, the kind needed when going through tall grass and the chance there might be snakes there.

They were laced, using the little grommets, all the way up. That fascinated me. The men tightened up the leg of their pants and straightened the pantleg inside the boot. The high boots were a good thing, also, when they went through heavy weeds or stubble fields.

The hired man Schmitz comes to mind. He was really "mixed up." He got paid, but never slept at our place. The strange thing about Schmitz was the way he dressed. He wore two pairs of broad-breasted overalls, wearing them to milk cows and muck the cowbarn. When the outer pair got crapped on sufficiently so they could literally stand up by themselves, no problem. -- He simply threw them behind the machine shed and bought an identical pair, putting the new pair underneath the other pair, wearing those two pair until the outer pair could stand alone. When I heard *that* I was glad he hadn't stayed overnight at our house. -- Everybody called him Schmitz though his first moniker was Martin. He reminded people that his name was Martin, not Schmitz.

EDGAR M. ROSENBURG

Must tell you, Reader/friend, about the cornfields and how the farmers can "hear" the corn grow. It sounds funny, but it really works that way. During the months of July and August when the weather is hot and humid, a person can indeed "hear" the corn grow. In the evening as the leaves unfold and reach toward the heavens they make a crackling sound. This is what the tillers of the soil hear. The oldtimers could hear it well, since the prairie was a much quieter place then. Nowadays there's a certain amount of interference. The corn could be heard growing in the evening as surely as we heard the birds singing in the morning.

One year my dad got the bright idea of "the gumps" weeding the corn. Dad had planted the corn at right angles so it could be cultivated from both ways and diagonally. Then when it got a little taller one day he "drafted" all four of us: Barbara, Carrie, Mickey and me out there pulling weeds. We put on our grubbies and we each had our own row. (What a deal!)

Dad had a row too. Mickey, being the youngest had a hard time keeping up, and Dad kept saying he had the "hookworms." I chuckle to this day about that. He had a sense of humor too.

I'll never forget the first time I noticed Dad pour his coffee into the saucer to cool, drinking his coffee from the saucer. That was so fascinating. I'd never seen him do that before.

And when he shaved he used the old-fashioned shaving strop with mug and the straight-edge razor, the ones found in antique shops and museums.

My dad made several trips to Michigan to visit Fred, Frankie and 'Clarie' in Flint. He came home with tales about riding the ferries and about the cities he had visited. He always kept a diary when he went traveling to see 'the girls' and Fred. Greatly impressed with the roads and highways was he, never forgetting to tell us about that.

When he drove down to Minneapolis and St. Paul he liked to eat at The Forum, he enjoyed the food there so much. Of course when they set it up like they do it does look appealing to the eye.

Dad did love to eat, like the rest of us, and how he loved his limburger cheese! It smelled so bad we kids couldn't understand how he got it past his nose, but he loved it. Every now and then he brought it home, and the piercing aroma permeated every corner of the house. This I recall when I was very small. By the time Carrie and I were in high school he didn't crave it so much.

Evidently dad had gone to Niagara Falls at one time. In the desk he kept this fabulous fringed brochure depicting the Falls from many different angles. We kids pored over that, and were careful to put it back in exactly the same spot where we found it. Otherwise dad would roar: *"I'm gon'na put my stuff under lock and key!"* And so it went.

And how he loved to talk the news and the economy. He knew what he was talking about too, keeping close tabs on the news his entire life. Whatever the news commentators reported on he knew about, sitting right next to the radio in his later years. He had cataract surgery on his eyes in his seventies and could no longer see well enough to read the newspapers.

One subject Dad shied away from was automobiles. Mechanics was definitely not his forte; he didn't pretend to know either.

The following yarn details another facet of my Dad. Carrie and I have bittersweet memories of riding to town for Sunday School. We dressed as fast as we could trying to get a seat on the right-hand side of the back seat. Outfitted in our Sunday best we'd pile in and wait for my mom. After waiting some fifteen or twenty minutes my Dad would grouse, bellowing: *"I've waited a lifetime for that woman!"* -- Mom had never driven in her life, and never went any place, unless Dad drove her.

Eventually Anna emerged from her domicile. She got halfway to the car, then turned back to the house. She had forgotten something. -- Minutes later she appeared again, taking her place beside her betrothed. As we went down the driveway she turned around giving us the sweetest smile I had ever seen. She liked to see us dressed so fine. We were all turning out.

When Barbie was still at home we girls all fit into the back seat while little brother Mickey rode up front between dad and mother. Barbie, Carrie and I looked like brightly colored posies. Dressed in our best clothes we were feeling good.

Out on the road things took a nasty turn. Picking up a little speed my Dad rolled down his window. -- He had one very bad habit: he "chewed." -- Now he spat out the open window of the moving car! I leaned over trying to dodge the tobacco juice, but invariably the breeze brought it back into my face! And onto my sparkling white blouse! Black spots spattered my collar, and sprinkled along the row of pearl buttons. Not a pleasant way to start the day! -- Sometimes the black bug juice still dripped down the car window, mute testimony to the whole mess. He hadn't rolled the window down far enough.

Usually running late even as a young girl I was sitting directly behind Dad in just the right place to receive the full blast of the runny black tobacco juice! -- Just one of life's little anomalies.

Carrie looked at me and did a silent snicker. She knew better than to titter out loud. Fishing out my hankie I tried to wipe the sooty stuff off. That left a smudge. -- There were times that Carrie got a spattering of the bug juice too. -- Dad didn't play favorites at a time like that.

I don't think we ever made a trip to Sunday school that Dad didn't spit out the window. We didn't squabble either. On the rare occasion that we might get into a small tussle Dad bared his teeth, clenched them tight and muttered: *"I'm gon'na get me a rope, wrap it around your waist, and let you run behind the car!"* Now I can appreciate the humor in it.

Dad always wore a felt hat, except in summer. Then he wore a dressy straw hat. If we touched the rim of his hat when in the car we heard about that too! It's humorous now, in retrospect.

In one corner of my hankie a penny was tied for the Sunday School collection. Most of the children gave pennies, but some of the (richer) kids put nickels in the plate.

We sat through Sunday school and church three Sundays a month. That was fine. But since this was a German community the fourth Sunday of the month the entire service was in the German language: hymns, sermon and liturgy. Motionless as if petrified we sat through the entire service not understanding a word.

Since my dad "chewed" he had a cuspidor next to his chair. And, Reader/friend, guess who got the job of cleaning it? -- Carrie and I did! We took it outside and scrubbed it with a brush, sloshing soapy water in and around it. Not a pleasant task, but we were so young we thought nothing of it. Those are antiques now, thank the Lord.

Sometimes my dad had the temperament of a caged cougar. -- When Carrie was four and I was almost six my Mom had found us look-alike dresses. They were ordered from the catalog and came through the mail. Carrie's was a muted orange print to match her dark complexion while mine was blue to go with my blue eyes. The dresses had Peter Pan collars, puffed sleeves and tied in the back. We tried them on; they fit us to a tee. Anna said we should go outside and show Daddy.

We found him in the yard. When we said these were our new school dresses he growled: *"Jah, now go roll in the dirt with 'em!"* We were so young we didn't understand the sarcasm. Many times his temperament was not the best, but most of the time he was pleasant, thank goodness.

Oftentimes when Dad saw me in the yard he would say something to me, but he never seemed to get my name straight, running through our names: "Frankie, Esther, Barbara" and finally he'd get to "Ruthie." (I never said anything, but thought to myself: "Doesn't he know my name?") When I became a Mother three or four times over I understood. I caught myself doing the same thing with my own. Guess all parents who have more than one child do this at one time or another.

For a couple years on Saturday nights Dad went to town taking only Barbara along. They spent the evening in Sleepy Eye getting home at 9:30. Dad had bought a box of Cracker Jacks for each of us kids left at home. Carrie, Mickey and I were waiting upstairs by the banister when they drove into the yard. Dad never forgot the Cracker Jacks, caramelized popcorn and peanuts with the sailor-boy on the box. They were only a nickel a box. We looked for the prize, ate the cracker jacks, then went to bed so we'd be up early in the morning for Sunday School.

After moving into town we walked downtown on Saturday evenings. In summer the high school band held a concert in the village park. The Sleepy Eye band members looked so fine in their snazzy blue and gold uniforms, brass-colored buttons with gold braid through the epaulets over the shoulder.

I would get a 5-cent ice-cream cone before the band started playing. One time I had gotten a maple-nut cone, and was walking past the produce store. The ice cream was melting, running down my fingers and hand. I licked it but couldn't keep it from melting, the night so hot. -- Moseying past the produce store I could hear the farmers saying: "It doesn't make a 'par-ticle' of difference…" That was the buzzword back in the forties -- "particle." Another thing the farmers said just for fun was: "All the meat around the pig's tail is pork!" That always got a laugh.

The Sleepy Eye merchants held a drawing on Saturday nights as an incentive to get more people into town. Top prize was $15. Second prize was $10., and third was $5. My mom's name was drawn twice, but she had stayed home and gone to bed early so couldn't cash in.

Dad's expressions were cute too. In winter when the weather got down below zero he would say, and I quote: *"It's cold enough to freeze the tail off a brass monkey!"* I can still laugh about that. -- If he wanted something done in a hurry he'd say: "Get on that job 'PDQ'!" -- (pretty damn quick). Like my mother, he didn't mince words.

Every now and again dad liked to go fishing with his cronies. He always brought home a mess of bullheads, a type of catfish. They were nice, as they didn't have a lot of bones. I recall him saying that fish was "brain food."

Dad had lived on the ranch for some forty-odd years. Fifteen of his seventeen offspring took their first breath there. -- Then he retired and moved to a small farm a short distance away. We were a quarter-mile closer to the school on the new place.

I liked to watch him "shoe" the horses on that place. By this time Dad didn't have many horses left. -- And all the younger farmers were into tractors, the new innovative way to farm.

I remember him sharpening the sickle for mowing on the little farm. He sat on the seat and pedaled to make the grindstone turn. He had set the sickle right next to the horse tank.

We kids did the egg-gathering on the little farm. We took the eggs over to the horse tank to test them for freshness, carefully placing them in the tank. If they were good they sank to the bottom. If they didn't go all the way down we threw them out.

It was on the little farm that Dad got the idea of making his fortune in cucumbers. There was a pickle processing plant in the next town, Hewitt, just four miles away. We kids were out in the pickle patch picking the prickly little things by 7 o'clock in the morning. The leaves were soaking wet with dew at that hour and made our hands itch like crazy. But we knew better than to complain. It was good discipline for a kid growing up, but I wouldn't want to do it for a living.

While we still lived on the Ranch towards the end of summer the threshing machine came rattling into the yard. To us kids it looked a mile long. These antiques now stand on the highest hills in prairie country, placed there to deflect lightening during electrical storms.

Every farm family had a threshing day. It was an unheralded holiday. Hayracks rumbled down the driveway carrying men in bib overalls with hay wagons set in motion by a team of horses. The empty hayracks clattered out to the fields coming back with heavy loads of whiskery shocks to be fed into the hungry mechanized monster. The threshing ring consisted of five or six families; farmers, wives, helpers. All came to join in the celebration. Even small children and babes in arms came, teenagers keeping a watchful eye on the "chilluns."

The ladies arrived with an array of cakes, and pies still bubbling with cherry juice through a lattice crust. The lemon pies did a little "weeping" but tasted delicious nonetheless. The women pitched in as if they were in their own kitchens. Some of the wives started peeling potatoes for the noon meal as soon as the coffee was perked. Preparing for the threshers and crew was a team effort.

At precisely 12 o'clock noon the threshers checked their twenty-five-cent watches. They lined up to wash hands and face in the chipped white basins on the bench by the pump, rolling up their sleeves in an effort to remove the chaff and dust. They sat at the ample table, with new red-checkered tablecloth, every chair taken. The farmers feasted on pork and beef roast, plates flowing with gravy and mashed potatoes. --After the men went back to the yard, shouting good-natured ribbing, the kiddies and teenagers sat down.

When everyone else had had their fill the ladies sat down for dinner, coffee and dessert. They then set about making sandwiches for the afternoon lunch. Nary a minute was wasted.

An exciting time it was, coming with a great deal of anticipation, leaving us with fond memories. The scent of grain and chaff was thick and hung in the air for days.

The last year on the ranch we were raking leaves in the fall. The leaves had fallen, blended colors of red, yellow and brown. We kids were cleaning up the yard while Dad cut dead branches off the trees. With this crackling bonfire going, Dad decided to make use of the fire. He placed a potato for each of us along the edge of the bonfire. We kept working and an hour later we had nice baked taters to snack on. They were charred, but the inside was tender and succulent. With a little salt and pepper out in the fresh air they tasted good.......

Things didn't change much from one year to the next in that rural community. When the Father passed on they didn't even change the name on the mailbox. The initials might be different but if the son was named Junior they didn't even do that. It was a wonderful, uncluttered way to live.

CHAPTER VII GOOD NEIGHBORS

Our closest neighbors, the Furstenbergs, lived just through the sparse little woods on our own side of the road to the east.

My dad and mom went over there to visit occasionally during the evening. They'd get cleaned up, Anna putting on a fresh housedress and combing her hair. She sat down and washed her feet in a basin. Then they walked through the little woods.

Fenwick Furstenberg, a thin man about Anna's age, and wife Edith walked back and forth to our house too. The Lindbergh baby had been kidnapped at that very time and when they came over we had fun listening to Mr. Furstenberg. He whined when he talked and we could hear him whining: "When are they gon'na catch those old *katnippers!*" We heard that over and over. Poor old Fenwick could never get it right. -- They were good neighbors though. -- Everybody neighbored in those days, borrowing back and forth. They had had two sons who had been grown and gone for years.

"Once upon a time" Dad had ridden along with Fenwick to Wadena, the biggest town in the area, some sixteen miles from the Ranch. They got to the outskirts of the town of four-thousand and Fenwick stopped. Dad looked around and commented: "You don't have to stop here, Fenwick. There's no stop-sign here." – "Course I do Ed," said Fenwick. "Look behind us, just see all the cars that are stopping!" That was Fenwick, a good neighbor, but a little out of step with the rest of the world.

Just a half-mile west of us lived our good friends, the Wickersteads. They, like the Rosenburgs, had never heard of birth control and didn't believe in abstinence. They had had "only" thirteen children. Mrs. Wickerstead's babies were born during the even-numbered years while Anna's babies came during the odd years. Both families seemed to believe that the more people to inhabit the earth, the more fun for everybody! And at the time I guess that was true.

The Wickerstead babies received the same treatment as the Rosenberg babies. He or she was given a tin cup and a wooden high chair that fit up to the table. When the baby was a few months old the Mother pureed potatoes and veggies with her fork, and the baby gummed the food until his teeth came in. When the child began putting his dish on his head they knew he'd had enough. He or she drank from the tin cup while he was being weaned so it was an easy transition when he was no longer nursed. In that day and age, breasts were for feeding the young, not for showing off!

Babies were not entertained that much in our family or the Wicks. The infant was brought into the world, cared for and moved on to a bigger chair, with catalog, when the next child came along. I guess they figured the whole world was that way and they may as well get used to it early on.

After the last little Wick arrived on the scene and had begun to glow Mr. Wick liked to say he counted the kids when they came in the door. When he reached thirteen he shut the door. That was one of the few things we had ever heard him say. He was a very quiet man; and very hard working. – And like the Rosenburgs, his offspring all absorbed the work ethic.

The "Wicks" had a black Shetland pony they called Prince. Alvina and Rosetta ("Vina" and "Setta") would get the pony out when we were there so Carrie, Mickey and I could have a ride. That was when I was very young. Later on when Carrie and I were in the middle grades at country school we'd go over there on long languid summer evenings. We played "Kick the Can" and "Pum, pum, pullaway." Fun, fun, fun!

Mrs. Wick was a sturdy-looking woman with brown hair. She wore it in one long thick braid over her shoulder. Like Anna, Mrs. Wick loved to talk, and did most of the talking for both herself and her husband.

Once Carrie and I hurried over to Wicks to borrow a cup of sugar. Anna was making a cake. There in the yard pecking in the dirt were these funny looking hens, speckled gray and humped over. They were "banty hens" and are quite common, I now know, but we had never seen banties before and thought them peculiar. -- The Wickersteads were in a different school district and we didn't see them every day, but they were good people and we were glad to have them living so close.

When we were in the primary grades there was a weird story making the rounds about a snake coming up from the South as big as a culvert! We kids shuddered at the thought of it. We wondered what size culvert they were talking about. -- After some weeks of hearing this wild tale we realized it was one of those stories fabricated to give folks something to say!

East of the Pioneer School lived the Rubelskis, my good friend Dee's parents. I stayed overnight with Dee often and we had many good times together. We were like two peas in a pod. -- Just beyond them lived the Schultz'. They had a cute girl named Dora. I liked this girl 'cuz she didn't "cotton-up" to the teacher to get good grades. We Rosenburgs took a dim view of anyone "buttering-up" the teacher.

The Schultz were colorful people. Dora's dad drove a shiny black automobile of the day, a Ford, always kept in top running condition and very shiny. Mr. Schultz sported a handlebar moustache. That really impressed me at the time.

The following story deviates from the truth a bit, Reader/ friend, but it was such fun writing I decided to include it.

South of the school on a crossroad lived the Cutters, a couple in the twilight of life. It so happened that old Cal and Cleo Cutter had a “boarder” but they didn't know it!

Let me explain: the boarder, a man about thirty, tanned and with a jaunty air, lived up in Cutter's haymow. He came down from his hideout only at night after Mr. and Mrs. Cutter were safely tucked in bed. After the shadows had lengthened and the yard had sufficiently darkened he crept around like a cat-burglar making his way down to the cellar and over to the smokehouse. In the cellar he helped himself to canned veggies, trying not to pilfer too much at once, lest he be found out. Then over to the smokehouse he stole, snagging a sausage or two.

Mrs. Cutter had told a friend in Sleepy Eye that the food supply was going fast, but it had been a harsh winter. She assumed they were eating more of the canned goods and smoked meat.

The boarder had fashioned a nice little haven for himself off in a corner of the haymow, hiding his food and few possessions over to one side under the hay. In summer with more people around he hiked into town, working a few odd jobs. Then come fall and cold weather he holed up in Cutter's barn again. Here he had all the comforts of home for nary a pittance! He figured he was the smartest man alive to have hit upon such an easy way to make a living. But he never disclosed to anyone where he lay down his head at day's end.

This continued “slicker'n spit” for a year. -- Mr. and Mrs. Cutter had been known for their gorgeous flowers and shrubs, but now in their declining years the roses and hydrangea bushes were not so lush. The farmer and his wife had arthritis in their joints and had problems weeding and pruning. The trees and bushes were overgrown, giving the place a seedy look. The boarder liked the seedy flavor; it gave him a place to hide.

Old Mr. Cutter had one Guernsey cow. He sat down at the cow and milked her outside. -- One day in early spring Mr. Cutter was out in the barn pulling down hay when suddenly a gallon-jug of cider exploded, spewing the fermented stuff everywhere!

At this point the boarder/thief "man-about-town" knew the gig was up. He was out'ta there! Mr. Cutter ran to the house for his "twenty-two," but by the time he got back outside the boarder was halfway down the long muddy driveway. He wasn't losing any time, but just to let the varmint know how he felt, the crusty old farmer fired three shots into the air.

When he investigated the vagrant's hideout Mr. Cutter found empty fruit jars in various sizes filled with advanced stages of fuzzy molds, ham-bones that looked like they had begun to grow again, garbage-filled glass jars, a calendar listing ladies' phone numbers, and mice!

The tiny town was buzzing with stories as the boarder fled the area. Some folks said he had fathered several children in the county. The entire story may never be known, least of all to the notorious "boarder." But there was a surprise ending to the story. This guy who had had such an easy life going for himself up in Sutter's barn had worn a purple neckerchief. Some people said he even showered with it on -- although how they picked up this particle of wisdom never came out.

Some of the saccharine little ladies in Sleepy Eye claimed that one of the boy babies born that fall at the hospital had arrived wearing a tiny, purple neckerchief! It was crumpled up at birth, but when the nurses got it dried and smoothed out there was no mistaking. It was a scaled-down version of the one the boarder had worn! Others said the baby arrived with a tiny rake in one hand, and a toy pitchfork in the other.......

It was a town like most small towns, where news spread faster than maple syrup on a stack of hotcakes. Some of the old-timers liked to see how far they could take a story without being sued. 'Twas almost surreal. That guy turned out to be like a "favorite son" and now was nearly mourned. When the townspeople gathered 'round the pot-bellied stove at the General Store they surmised he had gone to live in another state -- which was akin to going to the moon today.

Come summer the little old ladies liked to gather outside on their porches and sip lemonade out of tall frosted glasses. The topic invariably turned to the boarder. -- One little lady who wore her dark hair in skinny pigtails and liked the red rocking chair said in her prim small voice: "Maybe he'll come back and see *me* someday!" She'd get this faraway look in her eyes and smile. She knew it was never going to happen but it was so much fun to consider the possibility.

People said the boarder had done more for that town than anyone in half a century. The young girls were prettier, the people happier; even the economy had taken an upswing.

CHAPTER VIII THE THREE R'S

The schools were worlds different in those days, Reader/ friend. But I believe the learning that took place in the "one-room" school was as good as in this day and age, even what with all the new audio/visual aids and computers of today. Our subjects were Reading, Math, History, Geography and Language.

We Rosenburgs from Johanna on down to Mickey all attended the Pioneer School, a mile east of us. These are the little picturesque schools that dot the landscape now. I'd love to chronicle that. The teacher, Miss Weir, presided over grades one through eight. She was a young thing fresh out of "Normal." -- We all liked her. She was nice.

When I began first grade we learned to read from the old-fashioned Dick and Jane books. In my mind I can still see Dick and Jane running and playing with their dog Spot. That really takes me back..... I can picture the books and can almost tell you what color clothes Dick and Jane wore, probably the primary colors: red, yellow and blue.

The country school was a happy place with its own brand of atmosphere. Upon entering the room we were met with the smell of chalk dust. Here the younger kiddies learned their ABC's and how to get along with people. We had the usual bell in the bell tower, but it didn't gong very often. The teacher liked the small bell she kept on her desk better. -- This was the age of innocence, when the worst infraction committed was one of the older students tossing a spitwad.

It was a refreshing time in my life. There were roughly seventeen to twenty-five pupils in the one-room school with two to five pupils per grade. Classes ran seven or eight minutes long. My mind's eye pictures large maps on the front wall hanging down like the popular window shades of that era -- the mid to late thirties. The largest map was of the world. (We may have been small, but we were in touch with the world.) Along side that was the Minnesota state map where someone had drawn a heavy circle around *our* town, Sleepy Eye.

The map of the United States had us traveling all over the West, East, North and South. Our country consisted of only the contiguous forty-eight states in those days. Alaska and Hawaii would be added many years down the line.

Geography was everyone's favorite subject. Miss Weir held contests on Friday afternoons to see who could locate a certain river or capital city. And the first and second graders learned the major rivers and cities right along with the upper grades.

Silhouettes of two of our beloved presidents, Abraham Lincoln and George Washington took top billing on the front wall just above the maps. The presidents looked down on us to see that we were studying and staying in line.

The alphabet was posted on a white border which ran along a line high on the front wall, the ABC's written first in printing, secondly in cursive. Miss Weir had hung comely pictures of life at its best, matted with construction paper on the walls. The room was really quite "friendly" as my mother would say.

Our desks were fastened together by boards that rested on the hardwood floor. If Miss Weir wanted to move one desk she had to move four at a time. When a student grew too big for his desk, no problem. -- He or she was merely moved to a bigger one.

The desks had been sanded and varnished to a satiny finish, but the crudely drawn hearts and arrows had been carved so deeply they were still visible on the bigger desks. These were fun to focus on during long hours at school before spring beckoned.

In the desks' upper right-hand corner were holes that had held ink-jars for the old "dip-pens." Dip-pens were not used anymore. They had been replaced with the new "fountain-pens." Few, if any, of the students used pens of any kind. Ninety-nine percent of the time we used good old lead pencils. We did use fountain-pens for Penmanship Class, that I remember.

In the rear of the classroom hung a large globe, raised and lowered by a pulley device. Another apparatus showed the sun with "arms" reaching out to the earth and the moon, all made to exact scale. Some of the students couldn't get it straight that the earth revolved around the sun and not vice-versa.

After the morning bell we stood to pledge allegiance to the flag, and to our country! Then we opened our yellow songbooks and sang from the heart. "Oh, Susanna!" and "My Country 'Tis of Thee" were favorites. A little ceremonial to begin the day.

The hardworking Miss Weir wore other hats besides teaching. She started the fire in the morning; and swept the floors in the afternoon. The job of taking out the ashes also fell on her shoulders, as did all the janitorial jobs. She hoofed it to school early in the morning to get all these sundry jobs done before the students started stomping in. She kept a close eye on the children for cleanliness of hands and body and was their counselor, confidante and friend. She put in a full day!

The schoolhouse had been built on one acre. We had tree swings on the playground and a diamond for playing softball, although we didn't call it "softball"; we called it "kittenball." When in the primary grades I was really impressed with how some of the "big" 7th and 8th grade girls belted that ball!

I remember the day Katie Olson brought her dog, a German Shepherd, to school. That dog was so smart. When Katie hit the ball her dog ran the bases! The dog usually made second base.

There he sat until she hit the ball again. It was a kick! That dog had more manners than a lot of people. Katie brought her dog only that one time though.

In those days people combed their hair. We lined up for Anna before marching off to school. She took a giant comb with sharp tines and sliced into our ears like we were metal! The big comb jabbed our ears so piercingly they stung! She had no time to worry about how it felt to us. Yet, in her own way she was a good mother. She was always there.

My memory is clicking back. Now it is winter. In my mind's eye I see my big brother, Rosie, at school. He's sitting way up high on the stack of wood he and the boys had just brought in. The first bell hadn't rung yet. The split wood was piled high against the wall behind the huge furnace. Rosie sat up there grinning like a kookaburra watching to see what Miss Weir would say and do. His boots rested on the brown metal jacket of the gigantic wood stove. --We had trekked to school in fresh heavy snow. – (I now know the stove, with jacket, was not nearly as big as I remember it. Still in primary grades, to me the furnace looked awesome.)

Miss Weir was a sweet little thing. She was careful what she asked of Rosie as he was nearly twice her size. -- Funny, as a child I couldn't understand why it was called a "wood stove" when wood was what we burned in it. It never made any sense.

The young teacher liked the magazine *The Grade Teacher*. She asked the girls in the upper grades to hectograph off pictures for fun art activities. We put the master copy on this jelly-like substance in a pan like a cookie sheet, left it on for fifteen minutes or so. And, *voila!* we had our own copying machine!

In my reverie I see myself in third grade. The first-graders are up in front for reading class. The young teacher says this is the

"At family." Miss Weir believed in using Phonics, as did all the primary teachers in those days. All three first-graders said the words in unison.

Cat	Rat
Mat	Hat
Sat	Pat
Fat	Bat

The teacher took her magic wand (the yardstick) and pointed to the word. Sitting there mesmerized, I thought it might be fun to teach some day. A glistening star shone at the end of her magic wand. It was an enchanting time in my childhood. There was no yelling, no accusing, and no heated arguments, only the first-graders filling their little minds with the "At-family."

The morning sun slanted through the windows in glorious splendor. The walls were painted off-white with just a suggest-ion of pink pigment in the paint. When the sun streamed in, the walls took on a soft pinkish cast. It was very pleasant.

When I was in first grade the teacher had wanted me to sing a solo. She thought I had a nice voice. I was slated to sing "Smiles" for an afternoon program. Excitement was in the air! The whole idea thrilled me. So on program day all the parents arrived, looking so dignified and proud. Students were stepping up on stage to sing a song, recite a poem, or read a narrative. -- I was tingly, excitement caught in my throat.

The program was in progress. We students stood behind the curtain in a huddle. My turn came after Lloyd, a stocky 6th grader who played the harmonica. I was getting antsy. Then I heard the sweet young thing say: "Ruthie Rosenburg." Prancing to center stage I turned, took one look at that sea of faces, my chin began to quiver and I burst into tears! It was one of those things a person never forgets. That was my rendition of "Smiles." I can laugh about it now but that was a bad day.

The long walk to school but was as natural as breathing. School began at nine o'clock. The birds sat on the telephone wires and "had church" as we hiked to school. They sang the sweetest at that hour, and the air was fresh. We were truly blessed.

We walked through rain, sleet and snow as faithfully as the earth turned on its axis, taking the path along the lawn, down the bank, through the ditch onto the gravel road. Even in the deep of winter we marched. There were days of 30 to 40 below zero, the kind of cold that freezes your heels and breath, and attempts to freeze your eyeballs! Scarves were wound around our foreheads and chins, turban-fashion; over our noses we placed mittened hands. We still made our way to the country school under our own power, foot power. Rosie never put his earlaps down until the temperature dipped to minus ten degrees. He was the quintessential tough guy. On the rare occasion that he did, we knew it was cold.

If the sky opened up and rain poured down like God was sending another flood my Dad might take us to school, but that was a rare happening, maybe once a year, maybe less. -- We walked past Schlosser's cows and they had a big bull with only a barbwire fence separating us from the giant Holsteins. Most of the farmers had bulls in those days. We minded our "P's and Q's" when the black and white cows were up close to the fence and the road, holding our breath, not moving a muscle until we were well past the bull. Sometimes he would bellow and we knew he was mad. If anyone was wearing red we took off the offending garment and turned it inside out. We had heard that the sight of red made a bull mad and we weren't taking chances.

In those days some of the farmers had a few brown cows mixed in with the Holsteins, but all of our cows were black and white.

The culvert ran under the road and in early spring when the creek got full we put the lids on our Karo syrup pails good and tight, putting the pails in the creek on one side of the road. Then we ran across the road and caught our lunch pails on the other side! Fun! The other kids couldn't do that because they had store-bought lunch pails with sissy stuff on the cover: Superman, Snow White and Cinderella. Ours were airtight, so were better.

When I was in fifth grade the country school received surplus foods from the State. We received the large cans of grapefruit juice, mainly. That was our introduction to grapefruit. It took a little getting used-to as our lips puckered when we drank it, but we learned to like it. Can't remember any other surplus foods.

One year the school board decided we should have hot lunches so the mothers took turns making hot savory soup, delivering it to the school for our lunch. It tasted good on those anemic days of winter.

We didn't have "running water" as I said, but we had a reasonable facsimile at the school. One of the older students poured water from a pitcher into a basin and we washed our hands with soap, in the water running from the pitcher. That was our "running water." It was a smart way to go, and taught us a bit about sanitation. Using paper towels we dried our hands, all very sensible.

The water fountain incident occurred when I was a fourth grader. I was out in the cloak hall sitting on the floor eating my lunch, minding my own business. A couple boys began scuffling in the cloak-room and it turned into a real skirmish. I was seated next to the green water fountain, which stood about four and a half feet high. It held six gallons of water, the water staying cool all day. The 7th and 8th grade boys had pumped water to fill it that morning before classes began.

I was eating a peanut butter-jelly sandwich made with "homemade" bread when all of a sudden these fist-fighters knocked the water fountain over! It fell on my head and I saw stars! Putting my hand to my head I felt warm blood! A bit alarmed was I, but I could still think okay, so thought I was all right. Never did I tell a soul about that! Was afraid I'd get into trouble bigtime. Can remember it as vividly as if it were yesterday. It's amazing what all could happen during an innocent day at school!

Once Carrie and I promised Miss Weir we'd bring a sharp knife to school for an evening program. Carrie and I walked to the school that night all "dolled up" carrying the butcher knife. Dad was bringing Mom and Mickey later. I don't think we had said anything to my mother about the knife. We just took it.

So here we were skipping merrily along when I accidentally slashed my knee with the butcher knife! We got our hankies out to sop up the blood. It wasn't deep, mostly a surface cut, but did it bleed! And we were wearing white anklets! I still have the inch-long scar on my right knee to prove it. It almost scares me today to think of all the foolhardy things we did as kids! And I had a penchant for getting into trouble!

Many years later I taught second grade, and I knew all the tricks. The kiddies never got by with a thing! -- And I used the same rule with my own kids as I did then: "Be friendly, but firm."

In winter we wore long stockings holding them up on our thighs with worn out jar rubbers my mom had used in canning, and I have the varicose veins to show for it now.

On the school grounds we had the regular outhouses same as at home. Except that the school was a “three-holer” with a crescent moon carved into the door. Our privy at home was built with only two different sized holes.

Will never forget the time I was sitting out in the privy at school contemplating when a younger girl came out and sat down. She was not built slender like the Rosenburg girls. She was downright chunky, and when she sat down her young thighs spread out all over the boards! My eyes were in for a bit of a surprise. -- A few years later she trimmed down though.

When I went out to the three-holer in the forenoon I still remember how the sun slanted in through the rough boards, creating a shaft of dust particles clearly visible as I sat there contemplating life. -- The crescent moon in the door let in moonlight for evening functions. Of course looking back on those days gives the whole experience a rosy cast.

After a couple years the sweet young thing took a job in another district. Our next teacher was Miss Pug. She wore her auburn hair in the severe old style pug, hence the name. She always wore high-necked blouses. Rumor had it she had once stabbed herself in the throat leaving a vivid purple scar. There was a definite air of mystery about her. People said she had been married at one time, but no longer had a husband. Whether he had died or they had gotten a divorce, we kids couldn't know. (No one spoke the word “divorce” out loud in those days. It was only spoken in whispers.) “Grass-widow” was another term we heard and wondered what it meant.

Miss Pug was quite a presence in the classroom. She was the big wheel that rolled around, and we knew it, and she knew it. We may have been just the tiniest bit afraid of her. All except my big brother, that is. He wasn't afraid of anybody.

It was during Miss Pug's reign that I underwent a strange situation. One day at school I was in deep concentration over a test we were taking. I must have been in fifth grade here. Not a sound could be heard in the room except for a student jumping up to sharpen a pencil. Suddenly Miss Pug called on me, asking me what I was chewing. I innocently replied in the negative.

"You were chewing something. I saw you!" she barked, in her omnipotent way. Whereupon she insisted that I step to the front and "chew" for all the world to see. I was bewildered. There was nothing in my mouth, but to appease Miss Pug I dutifully shambled to the front and proceeded to "chew." Weird! I didn't realize until the next day that I had been chewing my own tongue! I never told her that, however. I figured the less she knew, the better.

Another negative involved the report cards. These were sent home every six weeks and Dad signed the cards. They were the size of a recipe card and were placed in a heavy paper sheath. This particular time -- I was in 4th grade here -- I had received a failing grade in conduct. Nothing like that had ever happened in the Rosenburg clan! At least if it had I wasn't aware of it. I was scared to death and didn't know how to handle it. (I hate to admit how "bratty" I was.)

So about 200 feet from home I conveniently "lost" my report card in the tall grass in the ditch. When my Dad heard *that he said I had better go back and find it! In fact he would go with me!* -- The two of us went back along the road and by some miracle of fate there we "found" the horrific card in the tall grass in the ditch exactly where I had hidden it.

Upon arriving back at the house my Dad took me across his knee and gave me a good sound "thrashing." 'Twas the only thrashing I -- or any of the Rosenburgs -- had ever gotten (that I know of). -- I felt there was a certain distinction in that.

Can't remember what all I had done to receive the failing grade. Miss Pug had caught me and my cohort, Dee, swiping apples off the tree at Krauses, a farmhouse located right next to the school. Somebody must have tattled because Miss Pug was standing on the cement steps watching us! The apple tree was just across the ditch from the road. How could we resist the forbidden fruit! I remember a "bellyache" I'd gotten from eating green apples some time later.

Another time I was on the receiving end of the teacher's ire; I've no idea what it was. Miss Pug "made" me stay after school for twenty minutes. I was so angry I had to walk home alone that I walked incredibly fast! Nobody waited for me and I had to hoof it home alone. Upon arriving back at my house I couldn't believe how fast I had walked. I learned at an early age that if you want to accomplish anything in life you have to go it alone, without help from anyone.

There was the time that Rosie rode his bicycle onto Krauses' yard. It was in midwinter but there was no snow on the ground. A zephyr had come along and dried up the snow we had had. -- Krauses had an unfriendly black dog.

When big black bushy dog saw Rosie he went slinking in his direction. He didn't even have the nicety to bark, only letting go with a guttural growl. Black bushy dog lashed out at my brother sinking his fangs into Rosie's succulent upper-thigh, tearing out a piece of flesh!

I don't think Rosie went in for shots. Anna made a nice soft bed for him on the floor next to the parlor furnace. There he lay for several days recuperating from the big bite. The rest of us trudged off to school during those cold clear cloudless days. In the mornings we stood there for a moment, books in hand, looking down at Rosie. He grinned up at us mischievously since he had a good excuse for getting out of a few days of school. That was my brother, always a step ahead of the crowd.

I surely looked up to him. -- When I was in the lower grades and Rosie five years ahead of me at the Pioneer School I received an autograph book for my birthday, passing it around for everyone to sign. The autograph book is no more but I still remember what Rosie wrote. (He was way ahead of his time on this.) He scrawled the words:

"I am a little pinto
I'll do all I can do.
And when my shirt and pants don't meet
I'll make my little skin do."

We Rosenburgs were rarely absent from school. But if we caught a bug and threw up Anna knew what to do to remedy the situation. We had linoleum all over the house. If somebody vomited on the floor she'd put ashes on the vomit. That neutralized it, making the job of cleaning it up easier. I have no idea how widely this was done, but it worked for us.

If somebody in the upper grades was absent for maybe a week or so there was the old "saw" that he or she had to stay home and sit on the stove because they had lost the lid!

I did a few constructive things in grade school: when in third grade I embroidered a luncheon cloth in pink and purple flowers with a black basket-weave for accent. The teacher taught me to embroider, and when I finished the embroidery she taught me to crochet. So I crocheted around the edges of the luncheon cloth with pink thread. We pupils sent these handmade items to the Todd County Fair in Long Prairie. I received 2nd prize and $3.00

on the luncheon cloth. Am going to bequeath it to my eldest granddaughter. Am sure she'll cherish it.

Singing class was a fun event, the whole school singing together. Often we sang along with the phonograph, as we had no piano at the school. I remember a picture of a dog sitting by a loudspeaker on the "music box," a Victrolla. The caption on the phonograph read: "His Master's Voice." We listened to the words and sang along. It was a delightful time. The teacher cranked it up. Then she put the needle on the record so we could sing along. Lots of nostalgia there.......

When Carrie and I were in the fifth and sixth grades at country school Miss Pug had some good ideas for Art class. One I especially liked was making posters using slogans of the day. We took our choice of slogans and designed attractive posters to make our point. Examples of these might be "A STITCH IN TIME SAVES NINE," "WASTE NOT, WANT NOT'," "HASTE MAKES WASTE," and "A BIRD IN THE HAND IS WORTH TWO IN THE BUSH." My good friend, Veda McKenzie did the artwork for "LIVE & LET LIVE;" that's a good one.

My Dad liked to preach the slogan: "IF THEY'RE GIVING SOMETHING AWAY TAKE VERY LITTLE OF IT." There's a lot of truth in that. Nowadays a popular slogan might be: "WHATEVER GOES AROUND COMES AROUND." That's one I like really well; but the one I think is the best for all time goes: "IT DOESN'T TAKE ANY SMARTS TO CRITICIZE."

When something involved art I was right there at the head of the line. I loved anything dealing with the arts.

I'd always been a great admirer of Veda McKenzie. She was in the same grade as Dee and myself. We had "races" at the blackboard, to see who could solve a math problem the fastest, whether it was addition, subtraction, multiplication or division.

Veda always won. She was a whiz at math and her answers were invariably correct. She did the math and put her chalk down first, but I liked her just the same. She may have beat me at math, but I could draw better than she could!

Beginning in fourth grade Veda and I sketched a picture together on the blackboard. I got busy and sketched in a pastel painting. Veda helped and we colored in the characters using the pastels. Taking the yardstick we marked in a calendar below the painting. For April we might do a young girl in her Easter bonnet, or a basket of colored eggs. All studying ceased while we did the painting. The pupils couldn't wait to see it.

Miss Pug shoved a couple empty desks along the blackboard with the calendar, but towards the end of the month it was mussed and rubbed off. Then it was time to wash it off and put on a new one for the coming month.

My final year at the country school I stayed overnight at Veda's house. I'd always thought she lived such a charmed life. She had black satiny hair, and had only a few brothers and sisters. I thought that was classy. And she was scholarly smart.

We walked the quarter-mile to the McKenzie's. Dropping our lunch pails on the kitchen table we went to her room. It was gorgeous! The wallpaper was muted shades of pink and purple stripes. I sat on the bed while Veda went to her dresser. Opening a drawer she took out a small white box showing me the contents: ten or twelve pieces of thick home-made frosting, the box lined with white tissue paper. Veda had gently removed the icing from chocolate cake, also luscious white frosting and a bit of pink. She offered me a piece; I chose the chocolate. She took a piece and carefully put the box away.

I had had such fun at Veda's house, playing kick-the-can after our homework was done. We played until dark, then "hung-out" where the yard light ended. It was a magical place, indeed. In bed we talked quietly for an hour before our eyes got heavy. The next day we skipped off to another day at school. Then it was home to the real world. I felt I was a better person for getting a glimpse into the world of Veda McKenzie.

The year my sis, Esther, was a "big eighth-grader" we had challenged Maple Leaf School, just three and a-half miles away to a Spelling Bee.

The boys and girls looked starched, having scrubbed and rubbed until their freckles were fading. The parents arrived looking so proud. There sat my folks in the students' desks, making amiable conversation with their neighbors.

The teachers from Pioneer and Maple Leaf Schools were taking turns pronouncing the words, as they became progressively difficult. One by one the boys and girls misspelled a word and sat down, but our Esther -- a mighty eighth-grader -- had not missed a single word.

She had waved her blonde hair with the curling iron that morning and dressed in her best clothes -- a short-sleeved white blouse with puffed sleeves and a navy-blue skirt. Everyone in our family knew how much she loved spelling.

The atmosphere in the classroom was becoming electric, words and letters echoing across the room as if propelled by invisible darts. The room was hushed as the audience kept their collective ears honed for a letter squeezed in the wrong way.

Finally there remained only two students standing for each "side." Esther and a young lady named Phyllis still stood for the Pioneer School, Dist. 59. The tension mounted, my Dad so proud his buttons almost popping.

Phyllis, the 7th grade contender, was given the word: *"idyllic."* She missed, putting an "i" where the "y" falls. She sat down. Then a male student on the Maple Leaf team fumbled on the word *"possession."* That left only Esther and her stout opponent, one Phoebe Wallingford standing. Phoebe had a round face. She wore a red corduroy jumper with white blouse, her brown hair in thick pigtails with red-plaid ribbons at the ends.

The suspense had built for twenty minutes. Esther spelled *"diarrhea."* Next Phoebe mastered *"mannerism."* Then it was Esther's turn. Miss Wallace from Maple Leaf turned to her and asked Esther to spell "sugar."

Esther blinked and wondered why she had been given such an easy word. She thought she had not heard correctly. Miss Wallace repeated the word: "sugar." Esther pictured the word in her mind. Doing a slight shrug, she turned directly to the teacher and pronounced the word: 'sugar' distinctly spelling "s-u-g-e-r."

A collective sigh was heard throughout the room. -- Esther had missed. -- Phoebe Wallingford was the big winner of the year.

We promised our Maple Leaf rivals we would be back the next year, the bigger and better to beat them. They hardly heard us as they skipped homeward laughing and bubbling as if Phoebe had sprinkled them with sugar and all they could do was laugh.

We had no doubt that Esther was the best, even though she didn't win. But Dad didn't let her live that down for months. -- I think sometimes people put too much importance on Spelling Bees. But you know, Reader/friend, they didn't ask me!

Early in December Ms. Pug received the Christmas seals, the proceeds going to fight tuberculosis. We looked forward to selling these; it was the kick-off for the Christmas season. I loved to see the new seals since they were designed by a different artist every year. Carrie and I were given a half-page each while Mickey got a quarter-page. These we sold for a penny apiece on the way home.

Our first stop was Krauses, the place where Dee and I had been caught swiping apples, but Mrs. Krause pretended she hadn't remembered it. -- *Also* the place of Big Black Bushy Dog of Rosie's bicycle fame. -- The dog never bothered us younger kids, however.

Mrs. Krause was a pleasant plump person. Her name was Lucille, but we never called her that. -- She had two black long-haired cats inside the house, "Tweedle-dee" and "Tweedle-dum."

Her kitchen was very "homey." She liked to make soup, and the aromas met us at the door. The soup had the windows all steamed up, while the sills boasted bright red geraniums. It was a happy place. I kind of expected the geraniums to hop down and start dancing around it was all so perfect. She had a place for everything and everything in its place.

This lady was so neat in her dress that she actually looked like a pin, all bright and shiny. When Mrs. Krause saw the new seals she squeaked: "My, they're 'purty' this year. And how you kids have grown!" She was really nice, buying a quarter's worth from Carrie and me each, and 10-cents worth from Mickey.

From Krause's we cut across a stubble field to our favorite place, Mildred Hey's. It was a half-mile out of our way, but we hustled along exhilarated about going to Mildred's. She always gave us cookies. -- We would just barely get inside the door and had say our "helloes" when Mickey would whine: "Oh, I'm so hungry!" As if on cue, Mildred headed straight to her teddy-bear cookie jar. She usually found oatmeal-raisin cookies.

We stood at the door chomping the big cookies. Here we eyed the dog dish under the reservoir: leftover cherry pie, or chocolate cake! Did that dog have it good! I-yi-yi! A fat short-haired white dog named Bingo, he could hardly waddle. But nobody worried about dog-diets in those days. We thought it strange that people let their dogs and cats inside the house. It didn't work that way in our family. Funny, I always thought that people who let dogs inside the house must have been richer money-wise. I have since learned that isn't the case.

Once in a blue lunar phase Mildred would take us into the parlor leading off the "front" room. We went through an archway composed of beautiful multi-colored glass beads making a lovely, tinkling sound as we passed through. It was heavenly. High on the walls of the parlor hung big olden pictures of Mildred and her husband Herbert when they were children.

The pictures were in heavy dark frames. The little boy, Herbert, wore a sailor suit with knickers and long white stockings. He looked to be about six and wore an expression that said he had sailed the world around. He folded one leg under the other at the knee. Mildred was dressed in a middy with a navy pleated skirt. Her long dark hair fell in lovely ringlets.

We loved everything about that room, the darkness, the purple velvet scarf on the organ and the tall three-legged table, besides the thin oriental carpet underfoot.

Once when we dropped in, Mildred sat down at the antique organ and played a few bars. It was an elegant place many years before that word became popular. The stop at Mildred's place made our steps lighter the rest of the way home. It was a fun place to visit, but we never wore out our welcome.

The annual spring picnic was the final gala of the school year. Our close neighbors, the Furstenbergs were there, even though their daughters were long ago grown. Also the Hofdahls, Freyholtz', Mr. and Mrs. Rubelski, Inez Denow, and her husband, and Veda McKenzie's folks, to name a few.

I can almost taste the lemonade served up in the big glass pitchers. Frost collected on the outside, lemon and orange slices floating on top. That was real lemonade. Donna Denow and I rolled the lemons in an effort to extract the most juice. Nectar was also served, made from the bottled concentrate.

Picnic day was the traditional field day. Miss Pug had planned foot races for the individual classes. I particularly remember the entertaining "three-legged" or sack-race. It was a blast, the students tumbling on the grass. Ms. Pug gave out the prizes.

And the food couldn't be beat! It was the good old-fashioned variety with everything made from scratch. One long table creaked under the weight of the desserts: chocolate pie, cherry, butterscotch, and apple pie. Also gorgeous white layer cake piled high with cocoanut, angel food cakes, mouth-watering sponge cakes, and giant-sized cookies.

Once I took a piece of chocolate cake, and found to my delight that the cake had "fallen" on one side. The depression was filled in with half-inch frosting! Quickly devouring that I hurried back for another piece, but that side of the cake was gone. Evidently others had made the same discovery.

Platters of ham, chicken, hot-dogs 'n buns, and with the coming of summer, potato salad made the scene. Some happy soul had brought home-canned dill pickles, and sweet pickles made with the tiny gherkins.......

CHAPTER IX INTERESTING PEOPLE

Some outstanding citizens lived in the little village. One such was the town barber, Red Westergreen. He was a tall slender man. What made this gentleman so extraordinary was his love for riding the bicycle. He rode his bike downtown to work even up into his eighties! It was like seeing a page of Americana painted by the brush of Norman Rockwell.

Another luminary was a kid. He was the chubby-faced child with a bottle of pop in one hand and a fistful of candy in the other. Patrons at the Sleepy Eye Tavern kept him supplied with these commodities. This kid had a toothless grin on his face at all times.

His real name was Jerry, but people called him "Butch." He had the distinction of receiving a full set of dentures upon entering the Army. All that candy and pop had taken its toll.

As Butch grew up he was never known to be at a loss for funds, finding ingenious ways of making a dime every day of his life. As a mere boy he went downtown to hunt for money. Four giant steps led up into the old red brick bank on the corner of Main Street, in the heart of downtown. Right beside the steps was a grate and a storm drain.

Butch would stick a wad of moist chewing gum on the end of a stick; poke it down through the grate hunting for coins. More often than not he would garner a dime, nickel or quarter. --Patrons coming out of the bank fumbled coins while putting money in their pockets, and Butchie was the richer for it, an innovative way of making a living for a kid.

When he was perhaps nine Butchie's boat sailed on Sunday morning at the dance pavilion. Naturally an early riser he was up at first light, walking to the eastern fringe of town to the pavilion. It was quiet as a cave in the dawning hours, even the leaves on the trees speaking in hushed tones after a rollicking Saturday night.

On a good day he spotted three or four half-dollars in plain sight spilt from pockets during the heat of a fight, the principles using only their bare fists. -- The ground beneath the steps was another lucrative spot. The lad's pockets hung happy as he trod homeward in the thin light of morning while Sleepy Eye slept.

This inventive way of making a buck carried over into that young man's life. That guy can smell money a kilometer away. He's the kind of person who could sell a hammock to an Eskimo, *in winter*...........

I also recall a little grandmother, Jenny, who was the mother to my half-sister (Helen's) husband. Jenny drove a little ol' jalopy with a rumble seat. -- Her car went all over the road. If someone mentioned to her that her driving was poor she would retort: "Oh, they (other drivers) can look out for me!"

This little grandmother pumped gas for her son, Kermit. Sometimes in summer she'd take the afternoon off and would crawl into the little jalopy and take a nap. There it was nice and warm. She curled up and slept. What a fun thing to do........

CHAPTER X TWIGS BECOME BRANCHES

Edgar's large family has developed into a powerful clan. My half-sisters are now gone, Martha having lived the longest, living until a hundred and two. (I must be honest. She was in very poor health the last two years of her life.) The others didn't live nearly that long. -- Albert, dad's first wife's son, married a teacher and apprenticed for a blacksmith learning the trade. He had his own shop in a neighboring town for many years.

My half-sisters Helen and Sally married and lived in the Sleepy Eye area their entire lives. -- Sally married a farmer who later served two terms in the legislature. He did a great job and was loved by his constituents. Sally and Bill traveled abroad often during his service as state senator. Sally told me that never in her wildest dreams did she think she would see so many foreign ports. -- They produced the most children in the entire clan, rearing eight children including at least two who went on to become college professors.

When my parents wed in 1914 the population of Sleepy Eye had been 459. In 1949 my high school class had taken a census of the town and it had grown to just over a thousand if my memory serves me correctly. -- Now at the turn of the new century it has shrunk again and is less than 600 as the young people have gone to the cities seeking employment. Sleepy Eye is a pretty town, most of the houses still painted white, the yards and flowers kept up neatly.

The farmers now have riding lawnmowers and air conditioned homes. -- But the most noticeable thing about the big farms (ranches) in the state of Minnesota is how they mow through the ditches far and wide. Every farm home has this wide expanse of grassy landscaped lawn, looking like a park. It's lovely. –

Tourists driving through the countryside have to really sit up and take notice.

Sleepy Eye has changed so much one would hardly recognize it. The theater was replaced by a Laundromat many years ago and is something altogether different now. The cafe where the teen crowd had congregated was razed many years ago. Such a lively place it was, the jukebox dancing around the floor with music and neon lights! That was the era of nickelodeons and long-playing records. In my reverie I see bobby-soxers sipping soda pop through straws wearing navy and white "saddle shoes" and flared skirts with a poodle in one corner. A bit of melancholy there.......

Those were the days of the 25-cent banana-split -- a colorful delicious treat served in an elongated dish with a banana split lengthwise and three scoops of ice cream on top. The confection was topped off with a choice of strawberry, cherry, pineapple, chocolate or maple syrup dressings. With chopped nuts over all. All this for a quarter. No wonder we call it the "good ol' days" -- (although sometimes a quarter was a hard thing to come by.)

A few businesses are exactly as they were "way back when." The mortuary looks exactly the same from the outside, every blade of grass standing at attention. The Sleepy Eye Tavern is much the same except the new owners have never had a license to sell "soft" liquor as it was in the forties. The decor is different too, but people still take time to stop and chat. That's the same as it was in the old days.......

The Greyhound bus still stops at Sleepy Eye on Highway 71.

Old hardwoods line the streets. -- One beautician in town charged "forties" prices until she retired in the nineties.

Esther Margaret -- of spelling bee fame -- was number six in this pod of eleven peas coming right after Frankie. She had a mind of her own and wasn't afraid to use it. Esther did much to blaze the way to high school for the rest of us. Dad felt that if the "gumps" had passed the 8th grade that was enough "book-larnin." Though he was an intelligent man he couldn't keep up with the times. -- The world was spinning too fast for him……

So when Esther graduated eighth grade she announced to Dad that she was going to high school. Well, Reader/friend, he felt she was needed on the farm to help Rosie, since the older kids had gone to the cities or Flint. He said to her, and I quote: *"Now Esther, you know we need you here more than 'they' need you thar!"* Well, Esther was not easily put off. She stood right up to her dad countering with a bit of defiance.

Blowing a wisp of hair off her face, she squared her shoulders, looked her Dad in the eye and declared: *"I'm going to high school!" And she did! Rosie drove her when that was possible. Otherwise she walked the three and a half miles.* And that was the end of it. I think Dad was caught in his tracks. No one had ever spoken to him quite that way, male or female. He didn't know how to take it, but I believe this time he realized that sometimes one's "young-uns" have a few ideas of their own.

Esther was one of the first "women-libbers" except that we Rosenburg girls wore make-up, bras and curled our hair. I thought it was terrific. She should have gone to high school. A couple years later Barbie would go. And we moved off the farm when I was in 6th grade, so Carrie and I lived in town and there was no question about it by that time.

After attending grade school Fred, Carl, Clara and Frankie went down to Minneapolis one by one working in the twin-cities for a while. They then followed the McQuillans – (good pals from across the road during their childhood) -- to more verdant pastures in Flint. They found work in the giant automobile factories there.

The four of them were all in Flint on December 7th, 1941 when the Japanese struck Pearl Harbor. That was 7 o'clock on a Sunday morning. The very next day, Monday, Carl marched down to the Recruiting Station and enlisted in the Navy.

All I remember about Carl is of him sitting on the kitchen floor against the wall in the evening playing the mouth organ. This was shortly before he made the move to Flint to get a glimpse of the world. We loved to hear him play. He was good.

After he enlisted we never saw him again. All we had was this lovely picture of him in his Navy uniform flashing this charming smile. One song I remember him playing on the mouth organ went like this:

"It ain't gonna' rain no mor', no mor'
Ain't gonna' rain no more.
How in the heck can I wash my neck
If it ain't gonna' rain no mor'."

In my mind's "ear" I hear: "She'll be Comin' 'Round the Mountain," popular at the time. Also "Little Brown Jug," and "Oh, Suzanna!" Very handsome was he, and talented musically. After boot camp he was assigned to the aircraft-carrier, the USS Wasp. I probably don't have to tell you what happened to the Wasp.

The ship was torpedoed in the Coral Sea September fifteenth, 1942, going to the bottom of the ocean. The larger percentage of the men swam away. Carl was not so fortunate. He could have been injured, not able to swim away. *It was his time…….*

We had received letter after letter that had been censored, clipped with a scissors. He had supposedly written sensitive material. The national slogan after the attack on Pearl was "Remember Pearl Harbor," and the Americans certainly did. Now, at this writing we remember the terrorist attack of September ll, 2001.

We can never go back to those days of nostalgia -- Carl playing the mouth organ. Dad kept saying he would come back one day, that our brother was alive, living on one of the South Sea Islands. But it would never come to pass. I read an historical account of the WASP. It stated that the sailors aboard the ship had been hand-picked. That sounds right. Carl had certainly been a young man to be admired. I don't think he had a flaw in body or mind. -- The article I read had quoted Churchill as saying: "Who says a WASP can't sting twice!" – I liked that, even though my brother had given his life.

After I heard the news, that our brother was lost at sea, I was in a depressed state for a month. Nobody knew it; I never told anyone. It was the same depression I had as an adult. At eleven years old this dark cloud hanging over my head was my constant companion. I could not shake it.

I'm bipolar, and can still remember when the depression lifted. Except for that one particular time I'd not had depression as a child. I always wondered if I would have that "condition" after the deaths of other siblings, but after that first death in the family it wasn't so bad. I did suffer a great deal of depression as an adult, but not so terribly much during and after a death as I had with Carl's.

Fred had sired three children, two girls and a boy. What was so engaging was that his first two children, the boy and then a girl, had birthdays on the same day exactly two years apart. It just happened that way.

Sid, Anna's eldest daughter, is now gone after a lengthy illness. She had been such a life-loving woman, playing bridge and leading a very full life, dedicated to husband and family.

It was so interesting when her children were born. They'd had a son and three daughters. Patrick, the son, was the eldest. What was so fascinating about the daughters was that the first girl was blessed with flaming auburn hair, the middle girl was flaxen haired, while the youngest daughter had the most gorgeous raven-colored hair I'd ever seen. I remember her daddy calling her "Pocahantas."

After Carl was killed in the war, and then Fred passing after a lengthy illness, Mickey, #17, was the next of Anna's children to go. He had survived Vietnam; then married and reared four children. -- While still a fairly young man he passed away of cancer, not living long enough to celebrate his fiftieth birthday.

Clara and Frankie are now gone. They married and lived in the Flint area their entire adult lives. Neither of them had had children although they would have liked to. I believe Francis tried to adopt, but at the time she was told she was too old. I believe the law has been changed at this time.

When "the Michiganders" came to Minnesota for a family reunion in the early eighties -- Anna was still living then -- they brought along their longtime friends, the McQuillan girls. I had the pleasure of getting to know them.......

Rosie resides in Las Vegas where his two youngest sons live. He was destined to go through some perilous times. His eldest son died in a car accident, and some years later the next offspring, a daughter, would succumb to brain cancer. Not only that, but he had just built a new home and within days of moving in, the house burned to the ground. Thankfully, no one was hurt.

He was quite the entrepreneur going into the trucking business and having his own fleet of trucks.

For several years Esther and her husband (who, incidentally share the same birthday) flew from Phoenix to Sleepy Eye for the summer. They then decided to live in Sleepy Eye year round where they could be closer to Helen and Sally. They moved into my mom's old house.

The old house doesn't look the same they have done so many renovations and have put in an entire new kitchen. It's quite lovely. That was the house we lived in when Carrie, Mickey and I attended high school.

Sister Barbara resides in Southern California and has four sons, all excelling at their jobs. She's best known for her trips abroad after her sons were on their own. She dearly loves her grand grandchildren, as well she should.

Carrie and her husband live in a suburb of Cleveland. She's enjoying retirement to the hilt, playing a lot of bridge and going to all the best movies. They are currently on a cruise through the Panama Canal. She was blessed with two sons and a daughter and is a doting grandparent.

I guess I would get the prize for having the most children in the least amount of time. How fast were they? Well, Reader/friend, how does four babies in less than two years and four months strike you? My first three pregnancies came swiftly, and the third time around I was delivered of twins. That's how they doubled up so fast.

My husband was a student at the U. of M. at the time. From these statistics one might think we had sex every night and twice on Mondays, but the truth was we did not. The doctor said I was simply a very fertile woman, and I didn't know that a woman was more likely to conceive immediately following a pregnancy. It seemed that all my husband had to do was hang his pants over the end of the bed and I got pregnant!

This circumstance did have the humorous side. After the twins arrived my sister "Francois" (Francis) who had never borne a child called to say: "I want the recipe!"

My husband was never a chauvinist, but he pushed out his chest after the twins were born and pretended to be just that. He boasted to his friends and I quote: "We had to sandwich our girl in with another boy!" Eight years after these first four were born we were blessed with yet another boy. At this writing all are living in the Northwest.

I've suffered a lot of insomnia with my bi-polar illness. Decades went by that I didn't get two decent night's sleep in a row. But I was young and got through it. During the sixties I suffered a nervous breakdown and have been seeing a psychiatrist ever since. At this writing -- am now in my seventies -- my psychiatrist has hit upon the right meds that work for me, and science has made giant strides in mental health in the last forty years. As long as I eat regular meals, take my walks every day and take my medicine I'm doing okay, even very well. I still have insomnia but have learned how to deal with it, and which foods to eat in order to sleep.

Nothing much ever happened in Sleepy Eye but there was so much to talk about we felt we didn't miss anything. – I know I'm looking at my childhood through rose-colored glasses, but having lived in big cities (Los Angeles) and small towns I've observed something. Most anything that can happen in a city can also happen in a small town, except that in the small town we're looking through more powerful lenses.

During high school I was busy babysitting almost every night, both school nights and weekends. On the rare evening I might be home, not babysitting nor on a date, my Dad would ask me to make popcorn. This I did, using the old black iron skillet. -- My Mother would have gone to bed by 8 o'clock. She worked hard all day and was worn out. She rarely sat down to rest and never took naps.

Dad would ask me if I had brought my history book home. That would never happen. History was what I disliked the most, although I like it now. The next night, without fail, I brought the book home. Dad pored over that. He didn't care whether it was Civil War History, World War I History, or any other war -- or even in between wars. -- As long as it was history he was happy.

I loved to wear skirts and sweaters in high school. The year I was an accomplished senior I had found a large plaid skirt with a tweed running through it. Was constantly looking for different sweaters to wear with the skirt. I always tried to save enough money to buy another sweater, but money ran through my fingers like water at the time. I couldn't hang on to a nickel.

Carrie and I applied lipstick at the mirror above my mom's treadle sewing machine. Dad, now retired, would comment: "Oh, don't put that old 'barn paint' on." Or, he might say: "Wipe some of that old 'barn paint' off!" Carrie and I never did wipe it off, but he felt better having said that.

Speaking of the fire-engine-red lipstick I remember the time my eldest brother, Fred, came home with his wife and second daughter. I was a married lady with four children at the time. When I went to the mirror to put on fresh lipstick Fred peered around the corner of the kitchen door and watched me! I had been just a little tyke when he left home, and he couldn't believe I was all grown up. -- We had a wonderful visit and my Mother whipped up her "can't be beat" potato pancakes! – It was on that visit that Fred brought home a lovely Holly Hobby plate for my mom to hang on the wall. The caption read: "Motherhood is kind and good." His son who lives in the Flint area has been given the plate at this writing.

Another thing my Dad admonished me and Carrie about time and again was: "And stay out of those soft-drink parlors!" Carrie and I never did frequent them much. We worked after school so didn't have time to run around.

One thing my little sister and I did religiously was to put sponge-rubber curlers in my Mom's hair on Saturday evenings so she'd be ready for church on Sunday. She couldn't lift her arms up high enough to do her own hair, but was able to shampoo it. She loved to have us comb her hair. Her scalp couldn't have been terribly tender because as we combed she always said: "Rake it." And she never complained that we were "raking" it too hard. Her hair waved easily and held the curl all week.

I was the only one of Anna's children to go to college, receiving the 2-year Elementary Certificate at St. Cloud Teachers College, now St. Cloud University. -- I worked five or six hours every night at a drug store downtown as I was paying my own way. My brother Rosie did help me with books and tuition. -- At that time my insomnia began; and has continued intermittently ever since. I taught a couple years at Staples, Minnesota, then followed my sister Barbie out to Los Angeles, subsequently getting a job, not returning to the teaching field.

Getting back to my dad, another thing Carrie and I heard him say was, and I quote: *"Time is money!"* We heard that a lot. -- He spent his days taking morning walks and listening to the radio. He still kept up with the news as much as ever.

Summer and winter found my brother Rosie down at the dance pavilion on Saturday nights on the edge of town. He was the picture of manliness in an impeccable white shirt, four or five buttons left undone at the top, sleeves rolled back. The pavilion held a certain magnetism. Music was playing; the rhythm was swaying, and drinks were weaving a stealthy course. Rosie was romancing his girl.

Later that evening suddenly everyone gathered at the door! A fight was in progress! There was Rosie in the thick of it, fist-fighting like you see in the movies! Blood spurted from the corners of his mouth, little rivulets curving around dripping down his white shirt, the shirt I had ironed myself, only hours before. How Rosie loved to fight! Soon other young bucks joined the fray, four or five guys throwing punches. Whether they knew who or why they were brawling was anybody's guess!

I think Rosie felt something was missing if he didn't get in a good fight on Saturday night. Luminaries at the Sleepy Eye Ballroom were: Avis, who loved to jitterbug and never missed a dance. Other bobby-soxers included my friend Dee, also Doris, Karen and Cathy. I recall a guy called Whiskey Jack and the twin Twelker brothers, Dale and Danny. In retrospect I know those were the best of times.

Rosie could be found at Balmoral as well, a dance club on Ottertail Lake. His onetime girlfriend taught him to dance there.

He had always been a great one to “party” and have fun, probably more than the average bear! He talked in his sleep, about this girl and that girl, calling them by name, rambling on in his dreams. One of us girls might say: "What, Rosie?" Then he would repeat it. We girls looked at each other and couldn't help but giggle. Little information was ever attained, his answers were so fragmentary, but it was fun.

Rosie seemed to date a different girl every month. When he reached the stage in life when men take the heavy step of marriage he was seeing a woman by the name of Jane, a voluptuous redhead standing five foot, ten. She was a knockout. Rosie was gaga over this gal. As Jane and Rosie saw more of each other he talked about this sister and that sister. She had one precocious little sister and a dog. (They counted their pets too.)

One day, in her breathy voice his fiancée asked him: *"Rosie, how many sisters do you have?" -- "Oh, about a dozen,"* drawled Rosie, real laid-back. -- He really did have a dozen, all beautiful, like me!

Jane wanted to count them; Rosie obliged: "Well, first there's Johannah, then Marty, Sally, Helen, and Hildie. Also Sidonia, Clara, Francesca, Esther, Barbie, Ruthie and Carrie. That's a dozen; not many people can make a claim like that!" Jane said it was indeed a nice story, but she couldn't trust a man who claimed to have a dozen sisters. It was just too preposterous! And it wasn't long before that relationship went south.

The Lanus sisters lived on the edge of town, to the south. I believe they had been teachers, now retired. They lived by themselves and were seldom seen around town. Their place had been a farm at one time as on their property stood a round red barn. It was now a hobby farm; all the fields had been sold off. Remaining were a few acres and the buildings. One Sunday night at nine o'clock there came a rapping on the front door.

No one else used the front door, so we all perked up at the rapping. Here stood the Lanus sisters. They said they would like to see Dad, and Anna ushered them into the parlor.

The Lanus "girls" as they were called -- they had never married -- exchanged pleasantries with my dad. They looked like twins, so much alike they were, in stature as well as personality. Luella spoke right up to Dad. "We heard you were a good bank!"

They had a personal check they wanted cashed before business hours the next day, Monday. They were going on a trip and wanted to leave before the bank opened. The check was written out for three hundred, seventy-five dollars.

I saw Dad shell out currency in that amount right then and there. Scales fell from my eyes I was so surprised to see Dad reach in his hip pocket for that kind of money! He took out this dilapidated wallet and just shelled out the money! I could not believe it! *(And there were times I was afraid to ask him for money for sanitary pads!)*

CHAPTER XI WINTER

Something we looked forward to in late fall when the trees were bare was that enchanting first snowfall. It was exquisite when sitting inside by a wood fire, snowflakes falling silently through the trees stacking up on the back steps. The red barn made a nice backdrop for the white snow, all very serene.

Along with cold weather came thoughts of making Jello. We had to wait for winter to make the wobbly dessert. We mixed the gelatin, put in the fruit, placing a lid on it. Then we set it outside in the snow! By the time dinner was ready, *voila!* We had Jello! And we completed this feat without the aid of plastics.

In winter we had wonderful fun! Rosie hitched Nellie to the bobsled, the horse in full harness. Rosie drove, with four or five of us girls and Mickey piling on behind. Nellie pranced all over the countryside, snow flurries everywhere, red and yellow plaid scarves and stocking caps flying in the wind!

Rosie drove down the main road a ways. Then he turned off next to Hey's property on a side road. We let the horse rest while we slid down Hey's driveway on small sleds we had tied to the end of the bobsled. When our fingers and toes were iced Nellie took us home. Going home she didn't lose any time. Once that horse was headed for the barn there was no stopping her!

One year it was a freezing November day and the old Midwest winter had settled in as if a snow-covered Sasquatch had taken over the land. Before school that morning I noticed the windmill with shiny frost crystals thick and sparkly in the sun. (During the night Jacqueline Frost had waved her magic wand turning everything crystal-white.)

The frost looked inviting but we had been warned not to lick it. I looked at the frosty windmill and couldn't understand why I shouldn't at least try it. Gazing at the forbidden frost I stuck out my tongue... and licked! *I stuck fast!* No way could I pull my tongue away from the frosted metal! This way and that way I pulled, but my tongue had become a permanent fixture!

I had to get myself disengaged from the windmill and off to school. In desperation and with extreme pain I very slowly and carefully peeled my tongue away, the epidermis of tongue remaining on the windmill! By that time my poor tongue was so swollen I couldn't get it back into my mouth! It was twice the size as before! Then I knew why we had been warned.......

We kids were home alone one January night when we had a monstrous chimney fire on the little farm. It was a rare occasion that our folks had gone out for the evening without us. Left home were Barbie, Carrie, Mickey and me. We were thinking about going to bed when all of a sudden the wood furnace began to "roar!" The draft may have been opened too far. We ran outside; flames were shooting out of the chimney! We were scared to death!

Why we didn't use the telephone I don't know. We must have panicked. The four of us set out on foot to the nearest neighbors west of us, less than a quarter-mile away. These people lived across from the Wickersteads, but they were young and had small children. As we ran, my heart was in my throat! Out in the darkness we kept looking back. Flames continued to shoot out of the chimney, sparks flying high into the sky! The roof looked like there were *patches of fire here and there! It looked like the whole house was going!*

Finally arriving at Froelichs we knocked. This man wasn't the least bit worried. He came out on the porch, a cigarette dangling from one corner of his mouth. He looked in the direction of our place and drawled: “Those things usually burn themselves out.” We waited around a few minutes, half-expecting the flames to take the house. It still looked bad… We looked up at the man, expecting him to do something, since he was so much taller.

After a few minutes the man said: “It looks like it's quieting down already.” We looked back at the house again. Sure enough, the fire looked less threatening. Smoke and sparks still spiraled towards heaven, but the flames were dying down.

The old house still stood, having come through the hellfire, her very being still intact. We hung around awhile, then decided there was nothing to do but go back home. We walked soberly. The place had a different meaning now. The old house had seen a lot and heard even more, everything from screeching and clamor to the sound of my mother making brushstrokes with her paintbrush. -- It was all history now, Rosenburg history. The next day when we awoke we had new respect for the old place. We were so relieved to know that our home was safe, now viewing life with new appreciation.

Some winters the snow got so deep that the snowplow couldn't get through for days. The plow was too busy. Then my Dad hitched up two horses to the hay wagon -- outfitted with runners. That was our transportation. We took the cream to town in milk cans. Here we received money for the cream, also cheese and good old creamery butter. Dad had worked at the creamery doing the books while Rosie took care of the farm; now Rosie had gone to the city and Dad was retired.

My birthday is in January. I remember the year I turned seven. Snow had fallen throughout the day and long into the night. When we got up in the morning the snow was four or five feet deep. -- Drifts had piled high around the house and the outbuildings almost to the eaves. Since I was only seven the mountains of snow looked much higher.

That year on my birthday I went alone into town with Dad in the horse-drawn sleigh. The Land O Lakes Creamery was our first stop. From there we went to the mercantile store where I was outfitted with a new pair of patent-leather shoes. What a fun birthday! -- Later that day dad shoveled snow making paths from the house to the barn.

When we had blizzard conditions -- snow with high winds -- Rosie tied a rope from the house to the barn so the men wouldn't get lost during the "whiteout." It was much like mountain climbers experience at high elevations. This was something we didn't want to mess around with.

When people were caught in a blizzard when driving they sought refuge at farms where they saw a light. When I was in my teens a girlfriend and I got caught in a blizzard. We had gone to an evening "show" and coming home we were caught in this maelstrom.

We drove as long as we could see the road. Then we pulled over to the side, staying with the car for a while. Later we saw a light in a window, maybe 200 feet away. Holding hands we waded through the snow towards the light.

We stumbled a time or two it was snowing so hard but we persevered, the light our guide. -- There we stayed for two nights until the roads were plowed. We had a good time in spite of being marooned, playing a lot of pinochle, and eating a lot of spaghetti, and were glad to get it!

Years later this woman became my mother-in-law! She was a good person; I guess we could say she was a mench.

Thanksgiving Day for the Rosenburgs was a big event. Anna baked parkerhouse rolls and pumpkin pies the day before. Her stuffing she made with raisins, especially tasty with goose. On the big day she prepared the goose and shoved it in the oven. Then we marched off to church, much like the pilgrims did. I personally like to do it that way, but with people moving around so much it can't be so simple as it once was. We always feasted on goose for Thanksgiving. I had never tasted turkey until we celebrated the holiday at the Hewers with my half-sister, Sally, and her family. *Those were Thanksgivings to remember! Turkey with all the trimmings, and a houseful of kids!*

For the Christmas holiday I recall Rosie going out to the woods and chopping down a tree. In my mind Christmas is tied up in ribbons, tinsel and all manner of glittering, shimmering things. Can almost "hear" the sound of wrapping presents, such a beloved holiday it was.

We had always celebrated Christmas (Jesus' birthday) with the children's service at church on Christmas Eve. We sang songs and said our "pieces;" the service was truly lovely. I see the little Rootkin seated on a small chair reserved for three and four-year-olds. Her chair was pushed so close to the enormous tree she could touch it! It smelled heavenly, the lights warming the twigs just enough so they emitted a soft fragrance of fir; the tree so tall, just inches from the cathedral ceiling. A star shone at the top, and the young people's group had hung a zillion icicles on the magnificent tree. The evening was as exciting as it could get -- Santa Claus would visit while we were at the program!

The program would not begin for some twenty-five minutes, but already there was standing room only. All the aunties, uncles, parents and grandparents were there to see the little heartzen (hearts) reciting their "pieces." The minister had started practice the first week of December.

I heard the minister speaking. Some of the children sang; others spoke rhyming poems. The little Rootkin patiently waited for her turn while studying the baubles on the enormous tree. After a little girl named Janice said her piece I walked up to the front and spoke loudly enough for all to hear, even those standing in the aisles.

At the end of the service we kids and the choir members received the traditional brown sacks. These contained an orange, ribbon candy -- peanuts, a Brazil nut and a couple walnuts in-the-shell.

Back home at the farm Anna lit the candles on the tree, a sight to behold! We sang a couple verses of *'Silent Night'* while the candles burned. Then Anna blew them out and we tore into the wrapped presents.

The year Carrie was three and I was five we received big life-size dolls with matching brown buggies. That was a memorable event. The next year our mother made new dresses for the big dolls from cast-off fancy duds of my big sisters. Mine was navy-blue polka-dots on a cream colored background. I still have the big doll. She's almost as old as I am!

The lad who would become my husband spent a major part of his childhood on Woodpecker Hill two miles north of Sleepy Eye. This lad and his grandparents were very near and dear to each other. They waited until the snow got real deep. Then they celebrated Christmas. Grandmama and Grandpapa put on their hats, scarves, and coats and buckled up their galoshes. Then they went out to buy presents for the grandkids. No doubt they ordered from the catalog too. Presents were hidden in the attic.

One Christmas the lad thought it might be fun to take a peek at what he had gotten. So the next morning he waited until Grandpapa had gone out to milk cows and Grandmama went out to gather eggs. With flashlight in hand he stole upstairs quiet as a cat. Pulling down the little ladder he peeked into the attic.

He got his eyes on a big tan cardboard box with black lettering on the side! Creeping into the room he gingerly lifted one corner of the big box. *And when he saw.....* He could hardly believe his eyes. -- Inside the box *was a train! So beautiful and shiny!* His eyes got big as sand dollars. He held his breath, sure it was for him. Then he let out his breath in one slow exhale.

He thought about running it, debating the subject in his mind. Now his hands were touching the shiny locomotive ever so lovingly. Before he realized it he had the round rail together! The engine he connected to the coal car, the yellow car to the red caboose. He found the key and wound up the engine to make it run. What stolen pleasure! He could hardly wait until Christmas morning when he could run the train for all the world to see!

Next morning he crept up the staircase again wondering if it had all been a dream. -- Again he found the tan box. The train looked *shinier than the day before*. Barely breathing on it he ran it just "one more time." And so it went. -- The hard part was trying to look surprised on Christmas morning, but the lad pulled it off with no one suspecting a thing, or at least they pretended not to.

CHAPTER XII ANNA'S LATER YEARS

After Dad passed, Anna, the matriarch, began fling around the country visiting her children. Dad had been eighty-three when he died; at that time Mom was a sprightly sixty-seven. -- Now she still had a lot of living to do. -- Never having been on a plane in her life she took to flying as if her ancestors had been a flock of birds, visiting children and grandchildren in Omaha, Cleveland, and Los Angeles. -- Also my family in Albany, Oregon besides my sisters in Flint. By this time she had her life well orchestrated.

She visited my family twice: first in Albany, Oregon -- and again when we built our dream house in the state of Washington. She flew out to see me both times mainly to "see my house." My friends said to me: "Oh, come on Rudy, she came out to see you, didn't she?" I laughed and acquiesced. But the truth was that she really wanted to see my house and she didn't mind spending the money to "get her eyes on to it!" We all were proud of her that she wasn't afraid to fly. The last time she flew out to see us she was 94. She made up for all her "staying home" years!

When Anna was in her eighties she was out in her back yard digging in the dirt when she saw something copper-colored. With spade in hand she bent over and reached down, discovering it was a penny. After brushing the coin off and cleaning it, imagine her surprise when she found it had been minted in the *very year that she was born, 1891!* I think God had a hand in that......

On the occasion that we might take my mother for a ride through the countryside she surely enjoyed it. Once we were in Minnesota vacationing with only our youngest child, a boy, along. The others were gone from home already. I could see my mom drinking in the sights as we drove along some of the unpaved roads. If we came to a farmhouse that had not been kept up well she might say: "Dat poor house needs paint." She loved to look at things with a fresh layer of paint. That's just the way she was.

When Sidonia's youngest daughter married I flew back to Minnesota for the wedding. "Sid" and her family were still living in Rochester, Minnesota at the time. After the ceremony they hosted a lovely dinner at the Holiday Inn, with dancing with live music. I was seated next to my mom. She commented to me that "all of her *flowers* were out there dancing!"

I had not gotten much sleep the night before and said to her that I was going to turn in for the night. When I asked Mom if she wanted to go too, she, at age eighty-five said, and I quote: "No, I want to stick around a while yet!" -- So cute!

Another thing she did when up into her eighties was inviting couples from church to her home for potato-pancake suppers, staying with her original menu of Polish sausage, pancakes, and applesauce. I suppose they reciprocated too. In the summer she served raspberries from her own patch, picking the berries herself.

It was during her "later years" that she told me a little about the German customs. She said that the German homemaker might say, regarding menu-planning: "For dinner we'll have potatoes: -- baked, boiled or fried -- then what kind of meat and vegetables?" -- Whereas in this country we plan our meals around our choice of meat. It was interesting to learn the difference between the two cultures.

There was the time that my mom fell asleep in her chair during her "later years." Upon awakening at 6:30 she did not know whether it was morning or evening. So she called Aunt Lucy -- her brother's wife -- who lived in the next town, Hewitt, four miles away, to ask Auntie what time of the day it was. -- She was a resourceful soul.

Anna was an enterprising soul as you know, Reader /friend. As she approached her ninetieth birthday this nonagenarian decided to make a quilt out of old neckties to mark the day. Edgar and the men in the family had worn ties for many years. There was no shortage of those; they lined the closets and trunks. Two of her stepdaughters, Sally and Helen, helped her. The quilt was colorful and attractive. A person could tell where Anna had done the stitching. Her eyesight was getting poor; and the stitches were not perfect but it was done with love. Mickey's widow was given the quilt.

Anna had planted so many trees and shrubs around her house it was nearly hidden from view. The birds loved it. When Stephanie and I visited there we awoke to all this chirping. It was like she was living in an aviary! Anna loved to hear the birds singing. It was not an unpleasant sound but I could never take it fulltime like my mother did.

When she went to church or to a special occasion she always wore her "breast-pin." She would get ready for church, then she'd say, "Oh, I need my "breast-pin.'" She'd run to find a pin; we'd put it on her lapel. Then she was ready.

My mother had more grandchildren and great-grandchildren than she could count. Otherwise she was much like the rest of us, with two exceptions. Firstly, she worked harder. Secondly, she had never worn pants. Until the day she died she put on a dress for the day. To wear pants was simply not in her character.

There is one other thing about her: She had never sat in the driver's seat of an automobile. -- How do you drive when you're nursing eleven babies!

When Anna was in her eighties and nineties she liked to say, and I quote: “I heal up overnight.” She always woke up refreshed in the morning ready for another day of living. She lived alone in her own home for many years after Dad passed. She liked the location, kitty-corner across the street from the church. When she could no longer negotiate the stairs she was moved into a nursing home. She was alive and well to the grand old age of 96. By that time she was tired. One Saturday night she went to bed and just slept away. She had been in the nursing home about eighteen months. -- She was a true legend in her own right. She is not with us anymore but she lives on in the hearts of her children.

ISBN 141207284-0

9 781412 072847